Managing External Legal Resources

To Ian

Best wishes

Dr A. Page.

Managing External Legal Resources

Ann Page and Richard Tapp

Published by ICSA Publishing Ltd
16 Park Crescent
London
W1B 1AH

Cartoons by Dave West www.accentukcomics.com

Typeset in Sabon and ITC Franklin Gothic by
Hands Fotoset, Woodthorpe, Nottingham

Printed and bound in Great Britain by
TJ International Ltd, Padstow, Cornwall

British Library Cataloguing in Publication Data

A catalogue record for this book is available from the British Library.

ISBN13: 978-1-86072-349-0

Dedication

This book is dedicated to Ann's parents,
Gene and John Page

www.cigroup.org.uk

Commerce & Industry Group (recognised by the Law Society)

Who are we and what do we do?

Commerce & Industry Group is an unincorporated association (UA) formed by in-house solicitors for in-house solicitors, and is administered by a committee. The UA makes representations to the Law Society, government departments and other organisations on issues that affect its members. The UA also organizes events for its seven regional groups:

North West, North East, Tyne Tees, London, Midlands, Central, Thames Valley

To become a member of the UA, solicitors need to complete a registration form either on-line at the group's web address or in hard copy requesting a form from the C&I National Office and returning it there after completion.

Membership of the UA is free

C&I Group Services Limited

C&I Group Services Limited ('the Company') is an incorporated body formed in 2001, limited by guarantee, to carry out the commercial activities of the C&I Group. The Company is controlled by a board of directors who work in conjunction with the UA committee and the regional groups.

Membership of the Company is by annual subscription and is open to:

solicitors; barristers; company secretaries; legal clerks; legal executives; foreign qualified lawyers working in the UK; and paralegals working in-house.

Individual subscription is £47.00 (inc VAT) and corporate subscription is £293.75 (inc VAT)

To become a subscribed member, visit our website: www.cigroup.org.uk, click on 'how to subscribe'.

The C&I Group is supported by a National Office based in the North West.

Contact us at:

Woodbank House   Tel: 0161 480 2918
80 Churchgate   Fax: 0161 968 1851
Stockport   Email: info@cigroup.org.uk
SK1 1YJ

Contents

Preface

In today's complex and changing world obtaining the best possible legal support from both internal and external resources is a constant challenge. During the past ten years it has become the norm for this to be provided by partnering arrangements of both internal and external lawyers in some form of service provision – whether or not formally documented.

In-house lawyers, in particular, are now expected to be leaders and not only manage their 'patch' but also provide strategic direction and continue to develop the best possible services for their organisation – hence the growing demand for cohesive legal services using the most effective combination of internal and external lawyers.

There is more pressure today on the need for both internal and external lawyers to be operationally and technically excellent, as well as to be seen to be delivering value for money. This also means that the 'partners' must have:

- *strategic astute plans* for evaluating and articulating the value derived from using both the internal and external resources. They must be able to evaluate and be credible about reputational and regulatory risk, contribute to the commercial success of their business, anticipate change and manage significant projects
- *a full understanding of the business*
- *clear roles and team working processes* for all parties with full understanding of authority levels. They must be skilled in planning and delivering a service that is value-enhancing. The value derived from having access to cost effective and knowledgeable in-house lawyers should not be underestimated
- *a communications strategy and process* for three-way (client, inside and external lawyers) and purely internal client communications which include a house style which is empathetic and commercial
- *documentation and technology* including good management information with excellent work-in-progress reports which show work priorities and action points in a way the business can understand

- and, last but not least, *broad competencies in a range of skills*, incorporating strong interpersonal soft skills including excellent relationship management. It is not what we do that counts, but how we do it. Therefore, Part II contains chapters which set out techniques for the 'how' where these do not fall naturally into the structure of the chapters contained within in Part I.

In writing this book we have drawn on our own experiences and in particular utilised as a case study the root-and-branch review undertaken in 2002 by Carillion plc of its own external lawyer network. Having always aimed to improve cost and service in other areas of the business, and to develop longer-term relationships with a smaller number of providers, it was a natural move for Carillion to think about its legal work on the same principles.

On analysis Carillion found that it used nearly 50 different law firms in the UK, but it had become difficult to manage the cost and logistics of such a diverse grouping. Lawyers are closely involved in much of what Carillion does, and its legal spend is significant. Carillion's lawyers work in areas where the law is developing, as well as those where disputes were traditionally the norm. There were concerns about the levels of service received, and whether the arrangements allowed Carillion to serve its own client base to the standard and pace required.

We believe that such a review worked well for Carillion. It took a multi-million pound legal spend and more than halved the expenditure whilst at the same time significantly improving both the quality and service, and reducing the number of law firms used by more than two-thirds.

Tribute must be paid to the members of the Carillion Legal team and the law firms in the Carillion Legal Network (who are listed in Further reading and resources) who have made it succeed. A word of warning, though: the partnering arrangements we have are not a template for every organisation. Every organisation is different – in its business, its people and perhaps most importantly its culture – and it is vital to design a legal strategy which will fit all three elements.

Conclusion

The in-house legal and company secretarial roles in any organisation are challenging, ever-changing and fast-moving. They are also something for which many of us receive little preparation, training or guidance beyond our professional development. As we said at the beginning, there is a growing demand to provide cohesive legal services using external lawyers, which in turn affects and influences how we manage our internal teams too. Therefore, this reality is also reflected in this book.

Remember, there are three kinds of legal department:

- those that make things happen
- those that watch what happens
- and those that wonder what's happening.

Before starting this book you may want to answer the following questions and then return to them when you have 'mined' this book to establish:

- Which one would you say that you are?
- Which one would your team say you are?
- Which one would your client organisation say you are?
- Which one would your external lawyers say you are?

Ann Page – Solicitor and Director, Beyond *the* Brief
Richard Tapp – Company Secretary and Director of
Legal Services, Carillion plc
August 2006

Acknowledgements

Business acknowledgements

Lord Thomas of Macclesfield for opening doors for Ann while she was Head of Legal at The Co-operative Bank p.l.c.

Sue Blake, Sue Blake Media and Matthew Sharpe, Challenor Group for their support of Ann in setting up her training and professional development consultancy, Beyond *the* Brief (www.beyondthebrief.com), and in writing this book.

John McDonough, Chief Executive, Carillion plc, for his support and encouragement in allowing so much to be achieved with ground-breaking legal resourcing in Carillion, and his consent to publish the case study.

Alison Shepley of Carillion Legal, who has worked with Richard on many of the issues and challenges set out in the book, and Anne Ramsay, formerly Senior Solicitor at Blue Circle Industries plc.

Keeley Chesworth of Carillion Legal, who contributed the case study for Chapter 17 of this book.

The members of the Carillion Legal team, the member firms of the Carillion Legal Network, and business colleagues within Carillion plc who have challenged and enabled the enhancement and development of the ideas set out in the case study.

The case studies and the Carillion documents within this book are reproduced by kind permission of Carillion.

The members of the Carillion Supply Chain team – particularly Sean Vallely – who brought their professional skills to us in working to establish arrangements for the Carillion Legal Network.

Dave West for drawing the cartoons included in this book.

Personal acknowledgements by Ann Page

To Rosemary Heslop for reading the various drafts and providing constructive comments and, last but not least, Richard Tapp, who was a joy to work with, in 'writing and producing the book that is in us all'.

How to use this book

The purpose of this book

The primary aim of this book is to make you stop and think.

Its purpose is to make you ask yourself the tough questions that need to be asked on a regular basis to ensure success:

- Am I delivering what my organisation wants and needs?
- If not, how can I change that?
- If so, how can I maintain the appropriate standards?
- Am I ahead of the game?
- Do I even know what my team and I are good at?
- Do I know what needs to be developed, and
- Can I articulate why that is?

This book is not intended as a text book, but as a prompt to enable you to ask the right questions and a guide to getting the right answers.

The best practice tips, techniques, exercises and documents are taken from both our experiences of leading internal legal functions and managing the provision of legal services from external law firms over a period of almost half a century between us. We have also included reference to the DuPont Model of managing external legal work, as we felt that this book would be incomplete without giving you some information on it.

This book aims to give you tips to enable you to fill any gaps you may have and to help your legal function to fulfil its potential within your organisation. It is not intended to replace relationship management skills nor the time and effort required to make managing external legal resources work effectively. Both external and in-house lawyers must work hard and diligently, and make allowance for the other, if true partnering is to be possible.

This book is intended to give you:

- *Tips and critical questions* covering the key areas in each stage of the process of considering your relationship with external lawyers – from allocation of work, through sourcing, procurement and panel reviews, to the management of the relationship and its end.

Each chapter follows the same format and looks at: planning; business perspective; clear roles and working processes; communication; and management, documentation and technology considerations.

When reading the best practice tips in Part I, do bear in mind they are not in any particular order of importance – it is for you to decide which is most relevant for your organisation and circumstances.

A *case study* is located at the end of each chapter in Part I of this book. Here we set out Carillion's experience in each area and outline the steps taken, showing how they relate to the key recommendations in each section, and try to share with you what worked well. We also show you some of the pitfalls we found along the way. Following the techniques in Part II, we set out a summary of Carillion's 2006 Legal Network Conference which dealt with service and communication topics dedicated to the 'how' of delivering legal services.

- *Techniques* which are about the 'how' not the 'what'. Again, the aim is to guide you with what has worked for us.
- *Tools with exercises* which will help you to think through some of the issues involved, and forms and precedents which you might find helpful in deciding what to outsource and what to keep in-house. These exercises have been used at Carillion and/or The Co-operative Bank p.l.c. and found useful in this context.
- *Further reading and resources*. We have listed some of the books and resources that we have found useful in helping us to be effective at managing external resources, whether these are specifically referred to in this book or not.

In reading our book, please keep two vital questions in mind, especially when completing the exercise tables or examining the documents to see what you can use:

- **How can I apply it here?**
- **Will it work for me and my organisation?**

We would welcome comments and/or details of your experience in using the recommendations, techniques, exercises and documents, and your own ideas and examples of best practice, which we will gladly credit in future editions of this work. Our email addresses are:

Ann: ann@beyondthebrief.com
Richard: rtapp@carillionplc.com

Part I
The tips

This part of the book covers the key areas in each stage of the process of deciding how best to allocate legal work – from examining the relationship with external lawyers, through sourcing, procurement and panel reviews, to the management of the relationship and its termination.

---

1   Allocation of legal work

INTRODUCTION

Whether to 'provide internally or buy' is a decision that is central to finding the most efficient way of resourcing an organisation's legal work. An understanding of your organisation's commercial needs, goals and aspirations will help you to decide on the best way to secure the legal capability demanded or needed.

In this chapter, we demonstrate the methodology involved in capturing the necessary information that will ensure you make the right decision for your business: to allocate the work to in-house lawyers, to external firms or other providers of legal services; or whether it is best to have it done elsewhere within the organisation by non-lawyers. Suggestions for drawing up a business plan are also provided and these will help you to anticipate and counter problems prior to putting any plan into action.

The processes described in this chapter will help you to gather all the facts and to prepare fully for identifying and standing up for what is right – the lowest cost is not always the right answer!

1. Understanding your organisation's perspective

Strategic astute planning

Plan. Remember that *failing to plan is planning to fail …*

Understand your environment. Before you build a plan it is essential to understand the environment in which you have to operate, both external and internal. Conduct the P.E.S.T.L. analysis (shown as Exercise 1 in Part III) with your team to assess the prevailing political, economic, social, technological and legal issues.

Understand your organisation. Understand the business and politics of your organisation – if you don't, who will?

Lead. Who is leading the allocation of legal work between internal and external resources if you are not?

Go back to basics. Don't forget the basic factors you need when collecting data in this field: economics, accessibility, knowledge, competence, and outsourcing know-how.

Mapping legal services to the organisation's strategy. When deciding what work should be outsourced and to whom, you may want to map the legal services to three key areas:

- organisational strategy
- corporate governance
- risk management policy and key processes

to ensure that these are aligned and you are adding value at the highest level. Exercise 2 in Part III – Legal activities to support the strategic plan – covers these important areas. If you don't feel comfortable reviewing these without including the 'day-to-day' service then you can add another section called 'operational support'.

Business perspective

List your business requirements. List your organisation's drivers, needs and *measures for success* in order to arrive at a framework on which to base your assessment of how to provide legal support both internally and externally.

Understand risk. Utilise and understand the risk drivers, policy and processes of your organisation and map how legal services fit against them.

This will also set the tone for understanding and achievement of the success required by your client organisation.

Understand your organisational needs. See the Commerce and Industry Guide to Corporate Governance, *Reconciling the Irreconcilable*, which contains some analysis of organisational needs from a corporate governance perspective. This may be useful to you in reviewing all legal support services required by your organisation (copies are available from the website www.cigroup.org.uk – including *A Fine Line*, which is the 2006 update on this topic).

Assess your legal services. Complete Exercise 3 in Part III – Legal services analysis. This allows you to examine the areas of law and drill down to specific tasks to establish what and how much the organisation wants to pay for.

Network. Join business or industry sector networking groups with your business colleagues (e.g. Chambers of Commerce, Institute of Directors, Confederation of British Industry and trade associations).

Benchmark. Seek benchmarking and current trend data applicable to in-house legal departments for your organisation and business sector from relevant networking groups or legal journals and publications.

Clear roles and team working processes

Consult. Consult all those who have a stake in the *value* delivered by your in-house lawyers – for example your colleagues, managers, all relevant departments, the board, the Chief Executive, and the Chair.

Review internally. Don't forget an internal review – identify processes that will reduce risk in the business and specialist departments that can be trained to be the first port of call for screening. Do not fall into the trap of thinking that lawyers need to do it all – train and trust your colleagues. For example, one of the ways to reduce support from a human resources department is to make managers more responsible for recruitment, disciplinary issues and dismissals. In this way, the business may operate in a smarter, better and faster manner.

Involve broadly. Do involve as many of the internal legal team as possible in any review and agree project roles as early as possible. Involving them from the beginning substantially increases the chances of success and buy-in for the new vision or modification of your current delivery.

Communication

Manage expectations. Develop your own strategy for managing your colleagues' or organisation's expectations of what should be provided internally and what can be managed by way of outsourcing, particularly if they have been set by external cost-cutting consultants or internal key people.

Agree a communication process. It is vital to agree a communication process both for your key decision makers and for internal clients – be prepared for requests for different processes for different colleagues but aim for one short headline version and one multi-tasked detailed report that appeals to the business clients, not just the lawyers.

Remember all the options. Do not confine the communication process just to the written format – do include face-to-face and team meetings to retain energy and momentum within the process.

Methodology, documentation and technology

Define your preferences. Do you gather data by electronic means and/or paper and/or meetings?

Align to your organisation's processes. What method does your client organisation use? Can you adapt this for your use without building a bureaucratic administration function or spending a significant percentage of 'legal' time preparing the documentation?

2. Understand your role – and that of your team

Please see Part II – Techniques, particularly Chapter 13 – Self-management and development and chapter 14 – Team working for partnering, and Exercise 4 of Part III – Personal assessment.

Strategic astute planning

Gain organisational insight. Do join in any strategic planning projects or leadership programmes run by your organisation, as these will give you valuable insights both into process improvements and into techniques used within your organisation.

Review your own role. Before looking at what you want to outsource, you may want to review your own role – whether this is as General Counsel, Head of Legal or Legal Director and/or Company Secretary. Does your organisation see your primary role as cost saving and/or process improvement and/or service function? In Document 1 of Part III we set out a detailed example of the very different roles carried out by in-house lawyers – multiple hats. Look at them, and compare these with your own situation. When you have done that, you may find it useful to work through Chapter 13 of Part II – Self-management and development.

Determine your strengths, weaknesses, opportunities and threats. Use Exercise 5 of Part III – the S.W.O.T. analysis – to determine the strengths, weaknesses, opportunities and threats affecting you. Use it with your team to identify your strategic assets – this will strengthen the team and provide understanding of the intellectual, cultural and operational strengths and weaknesses. It will allow you and your team to scope and assess the opportunities and threats, which might be political, economic, social or technological.

Understand your value to the organisation. Develop at least baseline knowledge of the key value of your legal department to the organisation and its unique selling point(s) at the outset of any strategic planning project – especially this one.

Balance your demands and goals. There must be a balance between operational daily demands and long-term goals. You need to schedule thinking and planning time in your diary to ensure that you can and do understand the value you bring to the organisation and ensure that it changes and develops as the organisation's needs and those of its Chief Executive change over time.

Business perspective

Decide on your strategic role. Make some strategic decisions – are you and your team going to do the 'big ticket' stuff or the 'bog standard' stuff? There is nothing wrong with either route – but you need to understand which you want to follow.

Don't just focus on today's demands. Most outsourcing decisions are based on how much legal work you have on, the type of specialisation required, and size of the team – this is the *wrong focus*! While these factors do play an important part, they only address the business exigencies and may not be based on value or the long-term goals and interests of both client and lawyers.

Remember to focus on how you deliver. When thinking about your value to the business do remember that it may value 'how' you deliver as more important than 'what' you are delivering. See Part II for some recommendations on techniques.

Work out why you're overworked. Do you have capacity issues? A silly question we know, as there are not enough hours in the day – but where do you have capacity issues and for what reason?

What do you cost, and why? How much does your in-house legal department cost (including salaries and overheads), and does this compare favourably or not with other similar companies and sectors?

What do the organisation's other functions cost, and why? Ascertain what is spent on the other areas of support expertise in your organisation – technology, business/management consultancy, human resources, finance, etc. and find out how they support their external spending and resourcing.

Clear roles and team working processes

Review your internal competencies. What are your internal legal team's strengths and weaknesses? If your organisation doesn't have a competency framework, at Document 2 of Part III we have included an in-house lawyers competency framework for your consideration. You may find it very helpful to use this as a basic framework and grow it for your circumstances as you develop.

Decide how you evaluate what you do. How do you and your internal legal team evaluate the importance of what you and they do?

Consider how you track your value to the business. How do you track and reward the value you and your team add to the business?

Build interpersonal skills. How do you build up your own and your team's legal and management expertise in interpersonal skills – with outside courses and/or experience? Is this experience gained with external firms on shared transactions? (See Part II for some techniques.)

What degree of delegation is right? How much can you or do you want to delegate to your internal team in managing the external lawyers? You might want to consider the use of specific relationship managers, as in the DuPont Model – see Document 3 of Part III (for specific techniques see Chapter 15 – Delegation).

White-labelling. Are your external lawyers assisting as their own firm or would you prefer that they answer as your department, or helpdesk – so-called 'white-labelling'?

Communication

Deliver on your promises – always. Be authentic and deliver what you promise – your word is your bond and an indication of your integrity. If your team cannot trust it, what message will this give to your business colleagues?

Drive outcomes. Turn knowledge into doing by making your meetings outcome-driven. Produce time-bound action lists and review progress regularly.

Share mistakes. Share your mistakes as well as your successes – it will make you more human to work for and with – if you are brave enough!

Methodology, documentation and technology

What management information do you have? Do you have good management information on all your activities? If you don't measure it, how can you evaluate or reward it?

Technology. What automated system solutions do you have or need to align with your organisation's standards? How well do *you* and your team use what you currently have?

Process and procedures. What legal, risk management or corporate governance process do you have that external lawyers will need to be aligned to?

3. Perspectives – organise your data and business case to support your plan for adding 'value' to your organisation

Strategic astute planning

The business case. Base your report or business case on finding the best balance of interests between all these competing factors identified previously. See Chapter 5 for some thoughts on leveraging value out of legal costs.

Preparing the case. Put together the appropriate business case, ideally using the documents, analysis or forms used by your own organisation.

Don't forget the softer benefits. Include soft benefits within this business case, e.g. 'confidence' and 'value' factors required by your Board and business managers and assess how these are delivered within the service.

Use the organisation's expertise. Utilise the expertise of your organisation's accountants and procurement teams for your business case for the provision of legal services.

Use core planning principles. Apply at least the basic planning principles to producing your business plan, whether you are a sole in-house lawyer or have a substantial team reporting to you:
- document the present position
- outline where do you want to be
- include an action plan and budget to get you there
- include a monitoring process to ensure that you know you are on track or when to revise the plan
- state what the measures of your success are.

Business perspective

Understand your market. It is your job to understand the business of providing legal services and the external legal market using your personal experience, peer group feedback, relevant books and legal journals, web sites and other information. Join legal networking groups – we suggest some examples on page 174.

Use all the resources available to you. You do not have to do this on your own, especially if this is your first time. Consider using an external consultant either for validation or guidance, for the whole process or parts. This is often how your business colleagues do it!

Determine your vision. Your vision for the role of the legal function – internal and external – is key. You must know what you want the lawyers to do and how they fit into the organisation.

Clear roles and team working processes

Buddies and mentoring. Set up a 'buddy' or mentor from within your organisation, or consider using an external mentor or professional coach to help you to evaluate your business data and provide a reality check, and review your value to the business.

Consult fully. As a minimum, involve the managers of your own department – or if your department is organised into different business units or technical sections, someone from each unit or section, as well as a 'buddy' or mentor from elsewhere within your organisation.

Communication

Define your goals. Decide how your proposed business case can enhance your own and your team's profiles within the organisation, particularly at Board level.

Present a professional image. Involve your communication and marketing colleagues in ensuring that any written information you produce is visually interesting as well as informative. It should also raise or sustain your profile within the business. See for example Document 5 of Part III – Legal Exposure Plan Framework.

Inform your team fully. Decide what you want to share with your own internal legal team during the build of your business plan. This will be especially critical for those people in your team who are not directly involved within the project. Beware – the grapevine will pick up any slack in your communication processes!

Be consistent. Implement your consultation, decisions and processes *consistently*.

Methodology, documentation and technology

Define your process. Decide how you want to record and retain this information; for example, Churchill apparently ran the country based on six lever arch folders. Do you want a full-blown client relationship management system or a combination of paper and technology? Work out what you need and will be comfortable with.

Use the organisation's technology. Does your organisation have an intranet – does your legal function? If so, ensure you are using it effectively.

Consider new technology. Consider if you need a matter management system – whether bespoke, standardised, computerised or manual – to measure and record:
- Who has conduct of which matter
- What matters are current at any time
- Whether the workload is a problem for anyone
- What costs are budgeted, work-in-progress, billed, and paid

Define your vision. Be clear about your vision for the future of legal services in your organisation – what you will do, and why.

Prepare a legal strategy. Prepare a legal strategy setting out in writing the key areas of what you do, why and how. As importantly, cover what you do not do. See Document 5 of Part III – Legal Exposure Plan framework for an example of Carillion's Legal Strategy framework which you might want to use. Some bases that should be covered include:
- alignment with the strategy and culture of your organisation
- your role – why you have an internal law department; what your external lawyers do
- which areas of law you cover internally and externally, and why
- instructions – who can instruct, and how

- how you measure and manage external and internal functions – your key performance indicators and service level agreements
- budgets (internal and external)
- charging policy and procedures
- know-how recognition and transfer between all parties
- legal risk – appetite and management
- arrangements for review of the strategy
- complaints handling.

Case study – Carillion's allocation of legal work

Strategic astute planning

The vision. We began by deciding what our vision would be for the provision of legal services within Carillion. It was clear that we needed to work within the context of a low-margin business dealing with numerous legal issues, which were often novel and complex.

Carillion's core values go to the heart of the way we do business. They are our differentiator in a difficult and complex market. We expect all our staff to work within them, and wanted our lawyers to do so too. Our vision had to reflect the need to do business in a way which fully supported and enhanced our value set.

We had to decide early on that the model would need to be able to cope with a significant demand for legal services, whilst at the same time seeking to utilise the commercial skills of our business colleagues to allow the performance of tasks within the business wherever possible.

The Legal Strategy. We soon began to develop a Legal Strategy – a formal document (see Document 4 of Part III – Legal Strategy framework – for a framework based on the Carillion Legal Strategy) which would later be adopted by the business. The Legal Strategy set out for all to see what the lawyers were for – and what they weren't. In our case, it covers:

- our role and functions – principally to enhance and protect the bottom line, and to preserve our asset base
- our philosophy – to have a high-quality, responsive, internal team co-located with our business groups, skilled in the core areas of law which we practise, and to source our remaining needs externally
- recruitment, retention, development and training

- the structure of the legal team
- the Carillion Legal Network
- what external resources we buy – and why
- the way we manage and resource our external work
- how we instruct external law firms
- key internal issues, including budgets, financing, cross charging, service delivery and key performance indicators, matter management, quality, managing know-how and legal risk
- our future priorities.

The 'provide internally or buy in' decision. We could only decide what to source externally when we had identified the work which needed to be done. We decided to concentrate our own legal resource on our key specialisms of construction law, facilities management and private finance.

Business perspective

Like many organisations, Carillion divides itself into business groups which each serve particular areas of responsibility. In Carillion, these now include:

- Business Services, which deals with national construction, facilities management and health, and provides integrated solutions
- Infrastructure, which deals with civil engineering, regional construction, and road and rail construction and maintenance
- the Private Finance function which provides specialist advice underlying that area of the law, and
- business entities which work internationally in the Middle East, Canada and the Caribbean.

Defining our requirements. We found managers within the business very willing to help us define what was required. We took business documentation, including business plans, risk matrices, the business risk assessment process, and structure charts and claims data. We reviewed what our competitors did in terms of legal support, and also looked at our own culture – Carillion set out to establish a clear set of business values which underpin all that we do, and it was important that our legal resource worked in harmony with them. Clearly, we also looked at the costs involved and collated information from as many sources as possible within the business on the past, actual and projected legal spend.

14

Clear roles and team working processes

Legal needs. We set out to review our legal needs – openly, critically and without preconceptions. We worked with managers throughout the business, aiming to speak to every major user of legal services across the Carillion group, as well as to the Chief Executive and the other executive directors. As the priority, we sought to identify our business needs. We looked at the legal risks facing the business, its future size and shape and the skills we had in-house.

Internal or external? We then defined what we should do in-house, and what was best outsourced, looking critically at our own resource, our strengths and weaknesses, as well as at the resourcing and support we had in terms of knowledge management, books and professional support. We identified that external resources were needed for a variety of reasons:

- to work on areas that we did not wish to cover in-house, such as employment, pensions, minor litigation and insurance work
- to represent our joint-venture and special-purpose vehicles, where funding requirements would not allow us to bring work entirely in-house
- to provide specialist advice in fields such as rail operations and property development.

Some 19 different areas of work were identified. However, we wanted more than a simple review of our legal provision; we wanted to use our legal teams – both in-house and external – to provide additional support in our core areas, such as construction, private finance and facilities management to help us gain competitive advantage.

Structural issues. We also identified that the structure and format of our internal department had to change. We had traditionally covered minor litigation. We no longer needed to do so and discontinued the function. The reporting lines for our lawyers varied. We standardised them, with a legal director being appointed for each business with direct responsibility to the Managing Director of each business group, but reporting to the Company Secretary and Director of Legal Services, and sitting on the senior management board of each business group.

Resources within the business. Carillion's business means that it has experienced professionals within its operations dealing with commercial matters, as well as bidding, tendering and contract drafting. A key desire in our process was to ensure that we could make full use of their skills by providing them with up-to-date precedents, training and know-how. We were also keen to ensure that the primary contacts for specialist areas such as employment, pensions and property development should be the subject specialists within the business rather than the in-house lawyers.

Communication

Consultation and briefing. Throughout, we kept our internal colleagues fully briefed, reported our position to them and kept them involved and onside.

Methodology, documentation and technology

The Legal Exposure Plan. During this process we developed an annual Legal Exposure Plan which was intended, for each legal function within our businesses, to bring our working relationships with our client businesses closer, covering in detail how we would bring the legal strategy to life, in areas such as:

- interaction with management plans, conferences and briefings
- relationship with business senior management teams
- training and development
- know-how
- precedents
- corporate governance
- risk management
- secondments.

An example of an Exposure Plan framework is given in Document 5 of Part III – Legal Exposure Plan framework.

Key learning points

1. **One issue which we could have easily underestimated was the resistance from some law firms to change. A key learning point was that we had to communicate with them as much as possible, and anticipate that they would lobby our colleagues within the business. The resistance to change graph in Chapter 11 is particularly relevant.**

2. While we needed to continue to focus on construction, facilities management and project finance law, we also had to recognise that our legal risks also meant we needed clear expertise in other areas of law to allow us to meet our strategic goals.

3. It was important to ensure that we involved and consulted fully – as a result we were able to implement an entirely new network of law firms with a very high level of buy-in and a virtually zero level of complaint from colleagues and users of the legal resource.

2 External sourcing

INTRODUCTION

You should have a clear understanding of:
- your organisation's needs
- what can and should be provided inside the organisation, and why
- and have clarified where you need help and why.

The question now is – who should you get help from, and how? This chapter deals with these issues.

Strategic astute planning

Do you have an internal process? Ascertain if your organisation has a supplier acquisition and supplier management process. If it does, then use it where it helps you. For more detail, see Chapter 3 – Procurement.

If not, develop one. Think of putting one together for your organisation, perhaps together with your supply chain or procurement department, where your organisation has one. If you are in from the ground floor, so to speak, then you can shape the development of the process and the role of your team within it.

Consider insourcing as well as outsourcing. Don't forget, if your needs are for legal work to be carried out within the organisation then temporary or locum staff (solicitors, barristers, paralegals or company secretaries) might be more appropriate than involving external solicitors. Legal recruiters and barristers' chambers are happy to discuss your needs here, and your external law firms may know of people who would relish time in-house, are between jobs or are potential secondees.

List all potential sources of supply. Do produce a list of the potential suppliers with an executive summary of the selection process you have adopted. You will be surprised at how many times in the forthcoming years this information will be revisited, possibly because of changes in management structures and strategy.

Business perspective

Consult your colleagues. Consult your business colleagues regarding their experiences and preferences for external firms and/or internal resources to ensure you match personalities as well as involving them in the selection decision process.

Conflict avoidance. You will obviously need at least two firms to avoid being conflicted, but otherwise you need to consider how many firms is it realistic for your organisation to have.

Be realistic. If you have a small budget covering six different topics including merger and acquisition work then what your external firms are actually competing for is quite small. Managing internal expectations about what savings can be made across that diverse and variable spend is crucial. *It is a viable decision to make no change at all if you cannot realistically improve the service or reduce the cost to the organisation.*

Manage expectations. You may also have to manage expectations if there should be a reduction in internal lawyers or external spend – and the implications on the appetite of the organisation for the assumption of risk about the activities which would no longer be handled by lawyers. Failure to take legal advice at the right time may itself be a greater risk.

Time recording. You may find it helpful to keep a record of the time spent on your work on the external sourcing project, including the management time taken in sourcing to give you an indication of the time used for this activity. How much detail you choose to document will be up to you and your resources, but it should be enough to identify what you have done – and perhaps to justify why you don't want to repeat the exercise too regularly.

Law is a people business. Even if you are not having a formal panel review (see Chapter 4 – Panel reviews), meet the individual lawyers who are going to be doing the work in your law firms as well as the relationship partner. This is especially important if they are not one and the same.

Clear roles and team working processes

Review the present firms. Ask the members of your team for their views on relevant external firms and review the history of legal work provided by any current providers of your legal services for your organisation.

Get a broad spectrum of views. Ask your in-house colleagues in your own and other organisations for their recommendations generally, and for specific expertise that your colleagues have seen demonstrated by particular firms and/or individuals. They may also have very useful information on all the little things that can annoy you, such as how prompt the lawyers are at returning calls and replying to emails, sticking to estimates, time-scales and plans, and complying with agreed relationship arrangements.

Use the directories and on-line resources. Back this up by checking with the Chambers and Legal 500 legal directories for specific recommendations for specific areas of expertise. Please see Further reading and resources at the end of the book for reference.

Communication

The procurement process. If there is no communication process for outside procurement, develop one for managing the external sourcing process with your internal business colleagues *and* your department.

Inform, consult, inform. Ensure, where possible, that everyone who may be interested in the use of lawyers is kept fully informed and consulted: they may well have valuable ideas and feedback, and if they are on your side they will be willing to own the processes. Roadshows may assist if the numbers to be involved or kept informed are significant. Please see the key learning point in the case study on page 24.

Supplier communication strategy. Have a strategy for early conversations with your current suppliers and potential suitors about your aims and the review process you are conducting to keep them onside, and to minimise any political manoeuvres.

Methodology, documentation and technology

Use the organisation's processes wherever possible. Often, you will find that organisations have their own selection process for suppliers. Ensure you use it or you will be forever explaining why you are different to everyone else.

Document your process. If you are time recording, or have a process for this project, then the whole team (if there is one) should be time recording.

Whichever process you are using, your system should allow you to produce appropriate colour graphs and charts of relevant data if your organisation finds these helpful.

Sourcing documentation. Any review or external sourcing of law firms should be run with supporting documentation on your decision points and process. You never know when you may be revisiting your decision for a new Chief Executive or management team and will want to repeat the process without having to reinvent the wheel.

Project management. Your organisation may well have the project management skills and technology which can contribute to your task here and be willing to lend you resources. For example, if you have specialist project managers or software programs such as Microsoft Project, or if you have available resources such as graduate trainees, secondees or leadership programme candidates they may well be able to provide an invaluable hands-on resource for the project. See the key learning point in the case study below.

Case study – external sourcing

Strategic astute planning

Supply chain. Like many large organisations, Carillion had an experienced supply chain function which was very willing to help in sourcing our new panel. We were able to use their standard Invitation to Tender as a basis for our tender document. In designing our Invitation to Tender (see Document 7 of Part III), we made clear that firms would be expected to sign up to a series of service standards in our written protocol. In considering them, we thought about the issues which are important – or irritating – about service delivery.

Sourcing decisions – one-stop-shopping or specialist resourcing? In thinking about the numbers of firms we wanted, we had to look at the areas of work involved because we were tendering the whole sourcing at once. In the end we came up with 19 distinct areas – some could clearly be shared, others could not. We expected to end up with between four and ten areas, some with more than one firm. This meant we deliberately sought out firms with expertise in particular areas, allowing us to look at 'boutique' firms or firms with particular expertise in one area, rather than go for a single source or 'one size fits all' choice. This was made easy for us because of the broad range of work we have – from day-to-day minor litigation through to specialist construction work and public company issues.

Business perspective

Focus on the bottom line. We clearly sought a significant reduction in cost – but needed to bear in mind that cost was a complex mix of issues, not just hourly rates:

- Does the work need to be done at all?
- Can it be done by non-lawyers?
- Is it cheaper to use a more experienced firm which does it more quickly despite higher hourly rates?

It is important to bear in mind that you may be a key client for some of your firms, and they may not welcome being asked to tender.

Dealing with the existing firms. We adopted a communication process to allow us to keep all our law firms up to speed with what was going on – and took a policy decision that all existing firms would be invited to tender. Due to the number of pre-existing relationships it was not possible for us to meet each firm individually to explain the process to them. We also agreed that where an incumbent firm was not asked to move to the second stage of our process, we would speak to the primary users of the firm within our organisation to allow us to give a reality check of our initial decisions.

We also found that firms were lobbying their existing contacts in the organisation – including at Chair level – and in one case claiming that papers had not been received.

It was inevitably the case that we were left with some unhappy firms – in our case we had an instance of a senior partner of one firm who visited following the process to inform us of his severe displeasure at being dropped. Recording the selection process involved is essential to give an audit trail to deal with questions afterwards.

Clear roles and team working processes

Identifying appropriate sources of legal work. We looked for recommendations for firms to invite to tender by:
- reviewing the firms we used already
- asking our in-house team for recommendations
- asking other in-house teams in the industry for recommendations
- reviewing Chambers and the Legal 500 (please see Further reading and resources).

Communication

Internal and external communication. We prepared a strategy to consult with and inform our key legal users – in Carillion's case more than 50 people; and were clear from the outset that they would be involved in the process.

Management, documentation and technology

Managing the process. We used a manual system managed through Carillion Legal, but did not time-record our time. We began with a simple project plan, setting out the proposed activities against time. It soon became clear that the scale of the process meant that getting the timing right was crucial – simply reading and reviewing some 50 proposals is not the task of a moment.

We project managed the arrangements ourselves within Carillion Legal. We then needed to ensure that we had sufficient time to consult users and clarify issues with firms. Even then, the process of bringing together presentation slots for the key areas of work – which we wanted primary users to attend – was a time-consuming and delicate process. The key here was perhaps to understand that it was likely to take a great deal longer than one might have anticipated – it was complex, difficult and needed to satisfy a multitude of needs.

Key learning point

Using a full-time project manager (if one was available) would have been invaluable and would have helped to shorten the process. Carillion now runs a Leadership Programme to advance the careers of chosen managers, and using one of these as 'an intern' to project manage the process would be something we would strongly consider if we repeated the process.

3 Procurement

INTRODUCTION

Having decided what you want to outsource and, in general terms, to whom, how should you go about it? In this chapter we look at the nuts and bolts of procuring legal services – how to go about it, what you should be looking for, and how to use resources in your organisation to help you.

Strategic astute planning

Use your procurement team. If you have a procurement department – which might be called purchasing, procurement, supply chain – use it. It can be on your side; it should be friendly; it isn't the enemy. Procurement departments are taking much stronger roles than in previous years; they contain professional, well-qualified people with up-to-date tools – a great resource.

Work with your organisation's procurement policy, not against it. Ascertain the details of your organisation's procurement policy – is your organisation:
- Seeking to reduce the number of suppliers?
- Defining specific criteria for suppliers – for instance in quality, sustainability, ethics and performance?
- Requiring key discounts for volume?
- Implementing policies about the procurement process itself – for example hospitality, lobbying, form of tender, who can buy in services?

Be clear about what you are buying. Using the model defined by David Maister in his book *Managing the Professional Service Firm*, you may wish to ask whether your requirements are for:
- **Experience.** You might want to buy work which can only be done by someone who is very specialist, has done it before and can replicate it

for you. Examples might be complex merger and acquisition work or brand protection

- **Expertise.** Do you need a rocket scientist – someone who can extrapolate their work into new and novel fields – new and groundbreaking work?
- **Efficiency.** In essence, commodity work such as debt collecting, high-volume commodity property work, franchising, regulatory work which has more of a process background and gives you peace of mind.

You may well want to approach different categories in very different ways – the firms, or at least the lawyers who do the work, will often be very different and will not respond well to 'one size fits all' procurement.

Business perspective

Work with the team. Procurement departments exist to buy in the organisation's needs as cheaply as possible, having regard to the need to maintain security of supply and value. Work with them to help them understand the balance of cost and value you and your internal clients need.

Rates v. resources. Don't let hourly rates drive the issue – in assessing cost the driver is the number at the bottom of the overall bill, balanced against what you get for it. Nothing in life is for free.

Use your organisation's outsourcing experience. Has the organisation already procured other professional services – such as audit, accountancy, insurance, estates – or outsourced operations such as human resources, finance or other work? Are there existing models, key performance indicators or service level agreements in place which have identified what your organisation needs? Don't re-invent the wheel unless you have to.

Don't assume you're unique. Don't assume legal services are so special that you can't learn from previous procurement work in your organisation.

Bear in mind it's costly for the law firm too. Understand that putting together proposals and making presentations is a time-consuming and expensive process for law firms – only ask for what you want and what will be useful to you; help them to give you what you want, otherwise you are asking them to cut costs, but not helping them to assist you.

Clear roles and team working processes

Define the roles. Define who does what. Your procurement colleagues might be willing and able to:
- prepare your basic request for proposals
- put out the tender documentation for you
- act as a contact point for queries and responses
- prepare an initial summary of responses
- help with assessment.

Be clear on what needs to be done – and what doesn't. Identify what you need or want to do in this process.

Lead the process. If you don't lead the project then you leave someone else no alternative but to do so – whether the procurement team, finance department or another player!

Communication

Define how you want to deal with your suitors. How do you want to deal with your prospective law firms? be clear from the start.

Contact arrangements. Identify contact points – you might want one for professional queries in your law department; one for practical queries in the procurement or supply chain team.

Timing and process. Be clear about timing and process. If you want proposals in a particular form – and at a particular time – say so and stress it clearly.

What do you want – and what don't you want? If you don't want reams of marketing information, CVs, newsletters and corporate brochures – say so.

Methodology, documentation and technology

Consider all the options for procurement. Consider what is appropriate to your organisation. Some of the tools now available include:
- internet procurement
- reverse auctions
- consultants who will run the process for you.

Use what fits your demands – not what suits someone else. Are your proposed methods appropriate for your organisation and type of work? Will they be counterproductive – or alienate potential law firms or mean that they will refuse to bid? How far do you see legal services as a commodity?

Consider your organisation's standard model. Do you have standard organisation procurement models? Are they appropriate or, at the least, can you adapt what is already in use? For example:

- Is there a standard organisation request for proposals?
- Has procurement already produced a useful summary of what the organisation is, and what it requires of its suppliers?
- Are there standard supplier assessment and measurement tools?
- Are there standard scoring processes which you can use?

Is there existing software in-house to help you? Is there already procurement software in place which you can use?

Case study – procurement

Strategic astute planning

Supply chain resource. Carillion's supply chain resource proved extremely supportive and very helpful in carrying out our review and appointment processes.

Before we started the legal review, we already had a clear policy in the business to reduce the number of suppliers, to require them to meet our quality, sustainability and performance criteria, and to measure what they did using detailed performance tools. It was very useful to be able to take this as a starting point, and to use appropriate business drivers from prior supply chain work – for instance to ensure that we had set up the quality, sustainability and performance criteria from a group perspective.

Range of work. Carillion buys a broad variety of work in different categories – our private finance work is often novel and at the forefront of development, whilst in employment we deal with issues which test the envelope of European regulation. At the other end of the spectrum, we have a run of minor litigation and estates issues which, whilst important, need a different approach and a different type of legal resource. We believe that the mix of law firms which we have, driven on the basis of giving work to firms which are good at it, actively want to do that kind of work for us and are hungry for it, gives us the best resource.

In considering our procurement options, we needed to understand the full range of issues, and the fact that the pace of change in the business had to be accommodated in our legal arrangements.

Business perspective

Outsourcing. It is often the case that one thinks of legal services as a special case, but in fact many businesses – including Carillion – outsource a number of functions, and the trend is increasingly to do so. The learning process involved in providing legal services in Carillion has also been used in buying in other professional services, including insurance and estates, and in putting together outsourcing arrangements for our finance and human resources functions.

It is important to bear in mind that outsourcing is not simply about putting everything to an external firm – it is important to decide the balance between internal and external resource, cost and efficiency. In our case, we deliberately chose to divide along the line of specialism and resource – but whatever the decision, it would have been important to ensure adequate, specialist resource in-house to manage the outsourced work.

Clear roles and team working processes

Processes. More details on the processes are given in the next chapter, but we found it very useful to work with our supply chain colleagues to:
- prepare the basic request for proposals
- put out the tender documentation for us
- act as a contact point for queries and responses
- form part of our assessment team
- develop the approach to the next steps.

Communication

Queries and responses. Having asked our prospective law firms for responses to our request for proposals, it was important to be able to respond to their questions. These varied hugely – from detailed questions about our legal requirements, to issues of process. They came from lawyers who knew us well – and from marketing departments delegated to prepare the presentation and proposal. We used our supply chain colleagues as a contact point for practical and process queries, and our own resource for professional queries.

Scale of response. We deliberately asked for four pages of response only – wanting firms to differentiate themselves from their competition rather than establish their ability to do the work. Despite this, many firms gave us much more information and lots of marketing details – sometimes running to many binders. As a courtesy we did read them, but in almost all cases they didn't help us in making the decision.

Methodology, documentation and technology

Proposal or auction? We thought long and hard about using internet reverse auctions for pre-qualified firms. We decided not to do so since we felt they would not drive value for us and would potentially alienate key firms. We considered the matter again when reviewing our firms at the three-year mark in 2005 – and stuck by our decision.

Carillion has a sophisticated supply chain function, which allowed us to adapt its existing processes and tools, including the request for proposals, summaries of the organisation's structure and requirement, measurement and assessment tools and scoring processes.

Key learning point

Our key learning point from the procurement process was to make full use of the organisation's internal resource. We had a professional and sophisticated supply chain, where colleagues were very willing to give their time, prior learning and systems to help us in our review programme.

4   Panel reviews

INTRODUCTION

The big question here is – Why are you doing this?

    A review of your panel of law firms, or the formation of the panel for the first time, can be very productive and produce significant improvement in efficiency, cost savings and service. However, it is time-consuming, demanding and can be expensive to run.

    Before you start, be clear that you want to do a panel review, and why.

Strategic astute planning

Remember your vision. 'Start with the end in mind' – Stephen Covey, *The Seven Habits of Highly Effective People*. What would a successful panel look like and what would be a successful selection process?

Be clear. Obviously the clearer the engagement process, the lower the risks to the business and the greater financial return and time saved not wasted.

CLO 6 Cs. The Chief Legal Officer (CLO) Programme has a system called the 6 Cs, which stand for:

- **Cost** – Are we getting value for money?
- **Competence** – Do they have the skills we need?
- **Commerciality** – Do they understand our ultimate business objectives? Both now and in the future?
- **Compatibility** – Is there a cultural fit? Can we work together?
- **Capacity** – Do they have the resources and are they scalable?
- **Credibility** – Will the business have confidence in them?

For contact details for the CLO Programme please see Further reading and resources.

Restrict your candidate numbers. Do not invite more than twelve firms for initial response in particular categories otherwise it becomes very unwieldy, and you are going to have a lot of disappointed firms if you can only select three to five firms. These firms may prove to have long memories next time you approach them.

Use manageable numbers for presentations and visits. Limit the number to six firms for presentations and visits per category – even fewer if possible.

How many firms should you have on the panel? We recommend that you have a minimum number of three firms on the panel unless you have extensive external work or budget.

Allocation is important. Think about panel allocation – different panels for different work or business types may be appropriate. One organisation we know has split its panel into three parts:

- Panel A covers initial transactions such as plot sales
- Panel B deals with acquisitions and disposals, planning and joint venture, and
- Panel C is designated for non-core specialisms such as employment, copyright, intellectual property and litigation.

Purchasing co-operatively. In the East Midlands, a group of local authorities has formed a consortium to buy legal services jointly, and to share information and know-how through EM Lawshare, which allows joint procurement and the formation of a number of centres of excellence in areas of importance to members.

Help is available if you need it. You do not have to do this alone, especially if it is your first time! Consider utilising external specialised consultancies to assist you or provide a complete service for audit or panel reviews. Please see Further reading and resources.

Don't forget sources other than law firms. Do not forget to consider barristers and their chambers' locums and legal 'factories' depending on your needs.

Business perspective

Stop. Think. Is this the right thing to do? Do you really want to do this? Does your organisation really want you to do this? If the external spend by the organisation cannot be counted in the millions for either a global or specific type of legal work then you may need to weigh up the pros and cons of this exercise or have an exceptionally simplified process to ensure best use of time – both yours and that of the external firm.

Manage expectations. Are you being driven by consultants/procurement or mismanagement by you about the 'value' you and/or your organisation are receiving from your external lawyers? Or has a change in commercial drivers necessitated a review? You really need to know, otherwise you will not meet the organisation's needs let alone its expectations.

Clear roles and team working processes

Manage your colleagues. Your organisation's key people need to be managed even more carefully than you manage this process. Be aware and plan for 'heading off at the pass' any unrealistic expectations to prevent you being a 'hostage to fortune'.

Work with procurement. Agree roles and processes with your procurement department – the procurement professionals these days often control this process. See Chapter 3 – Procurement.

Don't expect easy answers. Be aware there are no soft, easy answers – going through this process once will allow you to improve your management skills to ensure that you avoid the 'big bang' approach as often as you can.

Communication

Briefing the potential panel members. Briefing documents should contain the following information:
- strategy and business objects of the organisation Chief Executive and/or the relevant divisions
- the structure of the in-house legal department and its people
- key business people
- any specific sensitiveness, e.g. technology, brand, finance
- knowledge and document management
- performance measurement and appraisal systems
- added value and the measurement process
- working with third-party suppliers, if appropriate
- position with other panel members
- process, presentation and delivery

- the process for the tendering exercise: what – when – how
- specific questions, requests for information or measures for success you want the firms to answer.

Keep the documentation up to date. Be aware that you will need to continue to update this briefing information for the firms you appoint, and for your external law firms. You should plan to have the document periodically updated at least once a year if not on a more regular basis. See Chapter 6 – Beginning the relationship.

Use a steering group. Do not forget to have a steering group of senior key people both in your department and in the business to oversee the procurement process, and at some stage to 'eyeball' the final short-listed contestants.

Methodology, documentation and technology

Remember methodology and documentation required. The communication to the prospective panel must cover the methodology and documentation required from your target firms.

What is your preferred route? Are you going to use PowerPoint presentations or video conferencing or an extranet designed specifically for this task?

Law is still a people business. Don't just rely on technology and formal presentations – do give yourself a chance to meet them face to face.

Case study – panel reviews

Strategic astute planning

Criteria for review. It was important to decide the basis on which we wanted to carry out our panel review. Obviously, we wanted a high-quality service at the best cost – but what did that mean? At Carillion, we worked with our business and supply chain colleagues to define our criteria, and came out with a range of criteria against which we wanted to judge proposals:
- price and value
- market reputation
- brand

- experience
- accessibility
- service and delivery
- team members
- values
- cultural fit
- value-added services.

We realised that tendering the entire legal provision at once was a significant task. We started by examining whether we could simply re-tender some parts of the portfolio, but decided that because of the number of law firms used it was most effective to tackle the project all at once.

Business perspective

How important is an hourly rate? We were clear that the cost of legal services is a product of a number of issues – not just the hourly rate. See Chapter 2 – External sourcing. However, rates were considered, both because we use some work on an hourly rate and to give a measure of comparison between the fee structures of the firms.

How many candidates? We felt that this was a product of the breadth of legal work concerned, the type of work, and also the desire to ensure that we were giving firms who may have worked with us for many years a fair attempt at winning new work. At Carillion, we sought invitations to tender from more than 50 firms – but it is essential to relate the number you invite to the number you expect to appoint.

Clear roles and team working processes

Procurement. Procurement departments are often portrayed as the enemy in legal sourcing at the moment. They need not be – in our experience, and certainly at Carillion, they are staffed by professional, experienced, competent people who brought a great deal of value, expertise and resource to us. Our procurement professionals acted as the contact point for queries and for dispatch of the invitations to tender and receipt of responses from law firms. They also facilitated the process of assessing responses against our criteria and helped manage the presentations.

Communication

Invitation to tender. We used a formal invitation to tender framework to request proposals. Our Invitation to Tender framework is set out in Document 7 of Part III. We wanted to be clear that we had given everyone the same basic information, and that we had made clear exactly what we expected of firms, both in terms of technical legal standards and of the reporting, knowledge management, and ability to use information and resource to improve our business.

Methodology, documentation and technology

Process. We wanted to make sure we had set up a process which allowed us both to compare proposals fairly against one another and to involve all the relevant professionals within our business at an appropriate stage in assessing the best proposal.

We asked for initial written proposals, and the steering group used a scoring template to grade and decide who to invite for interview. If an incumbent firm did not make the grade on paper, we took soundings from users before deciding to put them through or not. At the presentation stage, we invited users to join the assessment panel and again used scoring sheets which were issued to each member.

Key learning points

1. We managed the procurement process internally, using a steering group of three lawyers and one supply chain representative; given the process again we would consider using a full-time project manager.

2. We learned that many firms were set up to respond through their marketing departments in a relatively standard way – we wanted bespoke answers to our specific questions. Doing it again, given adequate resources, we would have had individual meetings or calls with each firm to ensure they understood our requirements fully.

---

5   Leveraging value out of legal costs

INTRODUCTION

Once you have reviewed your needs, found the law firms you want and sorted out your resource requirements, what else should you be thinking about?

You may want your advisers to become an integrated part of the business and to work with you for years to come. You will also want them to build an understanding of the business which helps them to work better and more effectively, to everyone's advantage. In short, how can you leverage value out of your legal costs?

Strategic astute planning

Consider all the options on fees. When reviewing the financial elements of the 'value' received from your law firms, consider what role the following options may have:

- fixed hourly rates reviewed on a yearly or other periodic basis
- negotiated discounted standard rates as normal practice (discount rates are around 10 per cent in the United Kingdom)
- legal activities charged at cost
- region v. London v. national v. a blend of some or all. The regions can be 20–30 per cent cheaper but ensure quality is not sacrificed on the altar of cost saving
- capped fees
- blended rates across different types of work
- fixed fees per specific transaction or types of transaction
- performance-based fees
- value-based fees
- risk-sharing fee for mergers and acquisition and project work
- success fees

- transaction time savings due to deeper knowledge of specific work undertaken for your organisation or other service level improvements (but see below).

One approach is to look at return on investment. One organisation we know used this method and set up a system of primary and secondary investment categories. Primary was focused on governance and risk control, value-adding advice and transactional support. Secondary was focused on cost-efficiency and team effectiveness.

How important are the softer skills to you? What role will the softer benefits of value play within your success key performance indicators or other value you are asking for? How will they be accredited within this process? If you are not prepared to document or recognise the benefits, should you consider why are you asking for them? Some of your 'softer' benefits may be:

- value of trust and trusted adviser
- value of integrity
- brand synergy of the parties
- joint marketing or corporate responsibility initiatives
- cultural synergy of the parties
- management time savings
- rapid response times for advice and/or documentation
- anticipation of the in-house lawyer and/or organisation's needs
- process or commoditised workflow efficiencies/savings, e.g. improved contract structure and process, greater knowledge embedded in the people who negotiate contracts for the organisation
- an understanding of the economic impact of getting things right first time and done lower down the value chain
- open-book accounting
- internal law briefings for your team and/or the client
- sector and best-practice forums for your team and/or business
- secondments and trainees
- getting more work or a fixed amount of work might be a reward
- technology savings for new systems and/or upgrades to current systems
- 'freebies' – training and/or small transactions and telephone advice support.

Are you a profit centre too? What legal work can you charge third parties for? Do you have a system for logging this?

Compensation schemes. What financial compensation schemes do you have for the internal legal team and what plans do you have for those awkward conversations on reward between the internal and external lawyers?

Business perspective

Costs are a real issue. Understand client sensitivities on legal costs.

Risk assessment. Does your organisation require any type of risk assessment support such as:

- risk assessment forums for certain parts of the business or group
- risk of new and impending legislation alerts
- risk of adverse outcomes notices, or
- risk of overruns?

How do you value a value-added service? How does this support add *value* to your organisation and how will it be reflected in the price paid for services received?

Clear roles and team working processes

How do you assess the value of team working? What value does effective team working with your external lawyers have for your department and business and how do you reflect that in understanding the costs of providing the legal service?

Apportioning tasks effectively. Discuss with the internal legal team what the best methods are for apportioning tasks between them and the external lawyers to ensure cost effectiveness. For example, you may ask them to prepare a first draft versus amendments to a working document or be involved in particular stages of negotiations or advice.

Be specific each time. Remember, one type of process may not fit every joint transaction.

Communication

Be clear on your billing and authority arrangements. There should be a communication process for covering the billing and value systems, and in particular authority levels for particular types of transaction. For example, all banking transactions where legal costs are under £10,000 might be required to be signed off by the relevant corporate manager; above that the relevant lawyer may be involved as a second signatory.

These arrangements should be included in your protocol, contract or instruction letter governing the relationship between your organisation and your law firm. See for example the Draft Relationship Protocol at Document 9 of Part III.

Remember, it will go wrong sometime. There should be a communication process for when things go wrong.

Ensure everyone understands – not just you and the client relationship or contact partner. Every lawyer in the firm who works with your organisation should be briefed on the key elements of the arrangements between you – not just the senior client relationship or contact partner for example – using a Working Instructions Checklist such as that at Document 10 of Part III.

Tell your lawyers what winds you up. Last, but not least, you should communicate any sensitivities you may have, e.g. paying only for one lawyer to attend meetings, photocopying charges limited to a certain amount, or requiring compliance with your organisation's expenses policy. You may wish to refer to the Draft Relationship Protocol at Document 9 and the Working Instructions Checklist at Document 10 of Part III.

Methodology, documentation and technology

e-billing – size. Does the size of your legal bill justify an electronic billing system?

e-billing – scale. Does the volume of your transactional work justify an electronic billing system?

Billing and feedback loops. Some leading management consultancies use the billing system as the opportunity to obtain feedback by including questionnaires – would this suit you? You might also want to use it to trigger your Post-transaction questionnaire – see Document 16 of Part III.

Bills provide valuable data – use them. What do you want to do with the bills – apart from paying them? Do you want to analyse each one, just check it is in line with expectations and/or agreed parameters, or carry out comparisons with other firms on your panel for stage costs/time or total transaction cost/time? You might want to use an annual costs spreadsheet such at that at Document 14 of Part III – Annual fees spreadsheet – to identify the fees paid to each of your firms in each quarter.

Trend analysis. If you want to analyse the trends in your costs, consider a trends analysis spreadsheet. There is an example at Document 15 of Part III – Trends spreadsheet. This will allow you to see if your spend in particular areas is going up or down – for instance if your litigation spend is increasing, it will flag that you might want to review your risk management processes to see why.

Case study – leveraging value out of legal costs

Strategic astute planning

One-stop-shopping – or not? Carillion requires a range of legal services – from City corporate finance work to minor litigation; from specialist employment and pensions law to environmental work. It was clear to us that one size did not fit all, and so the Carillion Legal Network comprises a range of firms – from City Magic Circle firms to specialist boutiques, national firms and those in the regions – chosen for their specific expertise.

Fee and billing arrangements. We use a variety of fee and billing arrangements including fixed and capped fees; blended rates; performance and success fees, and elements of risk sharing. We also define hourly rates although the majority of our work is not procured on the basis of hourly charging. Our overriding requirement is that the fee represents value for money against the task.

Purpose of value-added services. Carillion uses value-added services to build relationships, to improve the efficiency of the provision of legal services and to help us work better, smarter and faster. We used commonality of culture and strength of brand as differentiators in the selection process, and have used a number of value-adding arrangements including:

- secondments
- briefing and training arrangements – both for in-house lawyers and business people
- improvement workshops – joint workshops with network firms concentrating on improving specific aspects of *the way we work together*.

Business perspective

The competitive environment. Carillion's business model requires complex, novel work – but market conditions mean that competition is strong and margins low. This means that frugality is key – and all legal work must be essential and must reflect value for money. We brief our lawyers on the extent of our margins – and ask them to ensure that their work reflects these.

Legal risk management. Our key role is about legal risk management, and we work with the Network in:

- identifying the top legal risks in the business – then taking responsibility for their management mitigation or transfer
- at the transactional level, using risk identification and registration tools – and ensuring that the issues they highlight are dealt with
- identifying, planning for and lobbying if appropriate on forthcoming legislation or policy
- putting in place know-how arrangements – training, precedents, procedures – to control and mitigate risk.

Clear roles and team working processes

Protocols. Our protocols use detailed provisions setting out what we are and are not prepared to pay for – on travel, copying, manning, expenses and

43

other incidentals. In general, we ask our lawyers to observe our own travel and hospitality policies. A Draft Relationship Protocol is set out at Document 9 in Part III.

Communication

Approval. Carillion has a detailed approval process – generally, work must be authorised by both the Business Group and Carillion Legal, and Network firms are aware that they should accept the approval as an appropriate safeguard. Our goal is to ensure that work is authorised before commencement and that budgets are set for each stage of a task. We do not want firms to do work which is not required, or to incur costs which we will not pay for – the approval process means that it should be clear what is needed and when, what cost we are prepared to bear and how we will pay for it.

Methodology, documentation and technology

Using technology. Carillion has not yet introduced an e-billing system but it is something we keep under review – we have also looked at processes which use third-party controls such as Lextend from Lexwiser or DataCert.

Key learning point

Law firms are willing and able to offer a range of value-adding services – but be clear that you need what is offered and put it to good use. For example, don't accept unfocused training – it will cost the law firm time and money to put together but will not be valued by the organisation.

6 Beginning the relationship

INTRODUCTION

So you have covered all the bases in choosing your favoured few – what next? The ground rules you establish now – and the methodologies and processes you implement – will govern how you will lead your colleagues, your organisation and your law firm in the relationship. Time taken in establishing what you want will be well rewarded. This means being clear with your firms so that they, and everyone in the firms who will work for you, understand what you want.

In this chapter we look at how you might record the relationship – whether in a formal contract, a confirmation letter, a service level agreement or a protocol, what it might contain, and how you should communicate the new arrangements within your organisation.

Strategic astute planning

Partnering models. There are no right or wrong partnering models – just pros and cons, and elements which will suit some organisations better than others. Partnering also means different things to different lawyers. The best of breed is the DuPont Model, but informal feedback from our colleagues is that the levels of expenditure of most organisations do not warrant such a formal and all-encompassing model. We have included a couple of tables in Document 3 of Part III – the DuPont Legal Model – to give you ideas about what might be appropriate for you.

Review your selection against your goals. Do review what you have learned, and agreed, at the final selection meeting against your original and new success criteria and look for any incongruence which may yet need to be sorted out. This should form the 'vision' and objectives for your new partnership.

Flex communication and risk profiling. Match your communication strategy and risk profiling systems to the external resource and work – be careful, as one size does not fit all.

Use a single process. Where possible, have the same internal delivery process for the external lawyers as you use for the internal ones, so it can be as seamless as possible for the internal client. Policies need to be as simple as possible.

Strategic planning. If you require any strategic planning for your legal work or transactions, ensure that this is covered in your documentation. See section 6 of Carillion's formal Draft Relationship Protocol – Document 9.

Business perspective

Review your progress against the organisation's requirements. Has the organisation achieved everything it wanted from the selection process?

If you haven't achieved your requirements, act now. If your requirements have not been achieved, do you need to place more emphasis on expectation management and implement an education process for your organisation's Chief Executive, Board and key senior and middle managers?

Check management is content. Ensure that your management is involved in the new partnership arrangements. If management has separate meetings with the law firms, ensure that you and they know what your role is.

Consider the implications of new regulation. How is the business going to access emerging regulatory themes for its risk management policy and processes? Is it going to receive training and to what depth?

Clear roles and team working processes

Competition can be productive. Do not be afraid of some competition between the internal and external lawyers, where it will keep both teams on their toes.

Familiarity can also breed contempt. At the same time there is a danger that increased contact will increase influence or over-familiarity. Both sides need to manage this effectively. Ignoring it could well breed resentment.

Be disciplined – ensure all processes are followed. Ensure that any specific relationship meetings are set up and in the diary and are reported appropriately, if you are using the DuPont Model or other similar model.

Social networking. Obviously you will have included formal meetings but think about social networking that might be appropriate – success parties, 'getting to know new members' lunches, etc. You may have a limit per firm so that no firm can appear to be exercising undue influence, and will need to ensure you comply with your organisation's policy on receiving entertainment from suppliers.

Be transparent. Do ensure that there is transparency. Be seen to be treating all firms equally and the internal team as favourably – no one firm must become the poor relation or be perceived as such.

Communication

Don't forget the basics. Key communication questions may still need answering following the completion of the tender process:
- review what and how you need to share and why
- understand and list what is absolutely vital, and what is rewarding to do
- what 'extras' do you have or want to do – be careful that you don't set up a bureaucratic process that needs constant feeding
- review your internal procedures – what works well which you can apply to your external relationships?

Use an agreed process. You may have decided your communication strategy and process. If not, you may well want to discuss with your selected firms as to how this is going to work in practice and any refinements required.

Kick-off communication is important. Depending on the number of firms you now have on your panel, you may want to commence the communication process with a series of separate firms, teams or business meetings. You may also wish to utilise the legal conference method that Carillion uses. See the case study at the end of this chapter.

Annual communication. Have you decided to produce an annual communication flow of information? If so, you may want to cover the following within that documentation:

- annual corporate strategy
- any changes to the corporate mission and vision
- key-people profiles on both sides
- contact points between the parties for what and when – single or multi party
- changes to any authority levels of the players or work remit of the firms
- meeting dates and key corporate dates
- reports – work – business – changes in structures
- the role of technology and any usage of intranet facilities
- service level statistical summaries of key performance indicators
- PR policy and process for dealing with media.

Methodology, documentation and technology

Defining the relationship. Having selected the source of supply, whether law firm(s) and/or barristers (and their chambers), and/or licensed conveyancer or litigation factories, then put in place a contract, confirmation letter or protocol to define the relationship. See the Draft Relationship Protocol at Document 9 of Part III.

Be proportionate. Match the document to the size of the task(s) being outsourced. You do not need a detailed instruction protocol for a single low-value matter; you do for a long-term ongoing relationship covering numerous or valuable matters.

Be open with your law firms. Headline key areas to be covered in the confirmation letter, contract or protocol with your law firm:
- financial terms and conditions should be prominent, not buried in the small print. In particular, be clear what you will or will not pay for
- governing principles – such as:
  o risk management appetite and policy
  o discretion areas of both teams
  o key corporate personnel and third parties where appropriate
  o ethical policies
  o brand sensitivities
  o communication policy
  o compliance policy

- o jurisdiction and, last but not least,
- o financial policies of the Legal Services Department or organisation.

See the Draft Relationship Protocol and Working Instructions Checklist at Documents 9 and 10 of Part III respectively for examples of the areas you may wish to cover.

Decide how best to document the processes – mutual understanding is key. You might use appendices or a manual to set out the detailed processes between you covering the governing principles set out above. Corporate precedents and standard terms of your organisation and your own department could be included in a 'how' manual or handbook. You will have to decide on what level of detail is appropriate for your particular circumstance.

Technology can be time-consuming. Do not underestimate the time and effort for ensuring technology synergies – now and in the future. Ensure equality – this will pay dividends rather than 'dumping' on the external solicitors the responsibility, costs and labour of establishing technological synergy. Remember this is a partnership arrangement and it may be appropriate for you to contribute something here – so establish what you are willing or able to pay for.

Case study – beginning the relationship

Strategic astute planning

Protocol. We wrote a formal protocol – a letter which we agreed with each Carillion Legal Network firm. The basic format of the protocol is the same but with variations for particular work types. An example of a Draft Relationship Protocol is at Document 9 of Part III.

Business perspective

The starting point. The panel review process within Carillion actually allowed the business to start the relationship on a very positive note. We were able to achieve more than we had originally thought possible – both in terms of the service standards and a reduction in cost that the new arrangements allowed us to achieve – not necessarily through driving down hourly rates but through better management, clear reporting, and structural arrangements and transparency.

Clear roles and team working processes

Carillion Legal Network Conference. We kicked off the relationship with a Carillion Legal Network Conference – a day-long event to which we invited six lawyers from each Network firm, the in-house lawyers and a representative selection of the key users of legal services from across the business. Our Group Chief Executive and a number of our business group Managing Directors gave presentations about their operations. We also discussed the prospective operations of the Network and had a number of small workshop sessions concentrating on the way the Carillion team and Carillion Legal Network firms could work together.

We have since run four Carillion Legal Network Conferences. The most recent conference focused on skills training and is summarised in the case study to Part II of this book.

Role definition. From the start, we thought it important to be clear that the in-house and Network resources were complementary. We tried to deal with this by setting out clear roles in the protocol and being clear in the first Carillion Legal Network Conference on who was to do what, and how.

Firm roles. Within Carillion we had different roles for different firms. We decided we'd use firms in core areas such as construction to provide additional resource in the areas of our expertise; in areas such as private finance to act for joint venture and financing arrangements – in each of these cases under the direct supervision of a Carillion in-house lawyer – and for supporting areas such as employment, pensions and property where the day-to-day contact and supervision is through a subject specialist such as a human resources or reward manager or a surveyor, with Carillion Legal providing oversight and review but not day-to-day management.

Reporting and review. We also use twice-yearly formal review meetings, and other visits to the Network firms – for example to speak about the Network and Carillion – but in our case we follow group policies on entertainment by suppliers so use social networking only to a very limited extent.

Communication

Communicating with the Carillion Legal Network. Carillion's communication strategy had several limbs:

- we issued company-wide updates setting out the fact the Network had been established and how it would work
- we worked with each firm to determine how best to define the relationship for their specialism – for example, for employment a number of kick-off meetings were held with human resources staff; with minor litigation, contacts were appointed within each business
- we posted clear arrangements on our Legal intranet, setting out who could instruct which firm and being equally clear that no new instructions could go to any other firm
- we made copies of the protocol available within each firm and within the businesses; some firms also issued simplified guides which were helpful to their staff
- we use a Working Instructions Checklist which goes to everyone who works with us within a law firm – setting out the key points of the protocol for easy reference.

An example of a framework Working Instructions Checklist is at Document 10 of Part III – Working Instructions Checklist.

Methodology, documentation and technology

Protocols. Our protocols cover the following areas:

- our values
- areas of work
- review and reporting
- who may instruct
- contacts and emergencies
- operation of the Carillion Legal Network
- case and matter assessment and review
- fees, charges and expenses
- staffing
- service standards
- documentation
- training

- conflicts
- media and other contacts.

See the Draft Relationship Protocol framework at Document 9 of Part III.

Matter management. At Carillion, we operate an off-the-shelf matter management system to track and record our work and the matters we outsource to Network firms. We considered in detail making this available for our firms, but decided that the complexity which it would entail did not justify the cost and the IT security issues involved. We do use formal extranets with a number of the firms, but these are considered on a case-by-case basis. We have recently reviewed whether a single IT platform would be beneficial and, for the moment, have decided against it – again on an analysis of the costs and benefits involved.

Survey and feedback. We use an online survey which allows users of legal services within the business to record their views on both Network firms and the in-house lawyers. See, for example, the Online survey feedback questionnaire at Document 12 of Part III and the feedback form at Document 13. This generates both a league table of firms and a comparison to the in-house lawyers, as well as a comparison sheet which allows firms to see how they have performed against the average and against their prior scores.

Key learning point

In some ways, beginning the relationship was the most important part of the process for us. It allowed us to set the tone clearly and rationally for the way we expected the relationship to work. We came to understand that unless we stated our requirements clearly, it was difficult for firms to understand what we wanted – each would come from a different point of view.

7 Managing the relationship

INTRODUCTION

'We are what we repeatedly do. Excellence then is not an act but a habit.'

Aristotle

In this chapter we look at the day-to-day management and measurement of the external legal resource – at key performance indicators, measurement survey tools and reports, reviews, and service level agreements.

Strategic astute planning

Lead – now and in the future. You will be expected to lead the management and to plan for the continuous improvements expected/required by your organisation. The key message is that you cannot just assume that you no longer require any strategy or planning once the relationships have been commenced with your partners.

Plan to build the relationship through realistic goals and clear measurement. You need to plan and work hard to build and maintain the habit of excellence, to set realistic strategic goals and targets, and to measure what is going on. In that way you may look forward to the relationship growing and developing.

Measure what matters to you. What is it that you want to measure, strategically and/or operationally? Some suggestions for you to consider:
- client satisfaction
- agreed performance targets and success criteria
- 'the extra mile' v. non-performance
- culture blending
- resource management – people (business and lawyers), time and teams

- process efficiencies
- financial or budget management or targets.

There are plenty of consultants, internal, management and/or legal management who could assist you in this process – but don't forget to involve the business and the law firms.

Don't try to measure too much. Once you have decided which areas you want to measure (strategic and operational) – then the next questions are:

- for how long do you want to measure, and
- how many target measures do you want to have per topic?

Do ensure that you only collect key performance indicator management data and don't get carried away by asking for absolutely everything you can think of unless you don't want to do any legal work!

Pain-sharing and gain-sharing. Think about rewards for good or excellent performance, and, more importantly, the possibility of penalties for non-performance. Do you want fees refunded, or losses covered – direct or indirect; or do you want the brilliant service that you were promised and have purchased? See the case study to this chapter and the Draft Relationship Protocol at Document 9 of Part III.

Business perspective

Which of your measures matter to the organisation? Are there any key performance indicators, service level agreements, management data or reports that should be made direct to the organisation?

Process analysis – who is responsible? Who is going to provide an analysis of completed customer relationship management questionnaires? Who is going to be involved in examining the data?

Clear roles and team working processes

Be clear about your role. Understand how you want your role to develop if you want to do other work. How much control do you need and how much can you live with – monitoring every transaction or troubleshooting the important barriers to efficient working and achievement of targets?

Client satisfaction is important. When you are measuring client satisfaction, ensure that the external key performance indicators you use can also be achieved by your own internal lawyers – don't set the external firm standards you cannot or won't want to achieve yourself. Be careful that the standards you set do not come back to bite you if you or your team are not up to scratch. See, for example, the Carillion online survey feedback questionnaire at Document 12 of Part III.

Use clear appraisal systems – treat everyone equally. What appraisal systems are you going to use for individual lawyers on the external and internal teams? Be careful not to set up more stringent ones for external lawyers than for your own people. Do remember to feed the appraisal information into the law firms' own systems for their people and ask the law firms for their input into the process for your own staff. Please see Chapter 16 – Appraisals and feedback – for further suggestions on how to conduct appraisals effectively.

Avoid a blame culture. Be careful not to create a blame culture and do not encourage 'backbiting'. If issues arise – and they will – having a system in place from the beginning that you can implement will ensure that personality and cultural clashes can be nipped in the bud. Don't blame the external lawyers for everything – you do not know when you may need them to pull out all the stops.

Blend the best of internal and external resource. How are you going to blend the best of both cultures of the internal and external teams? Don't forget this will take time and effort – it does not just happen by magic. Please Chapter 14 – Team working for partnering.

Project management. Consider setting up a *small project team* with representatives from the internal and external lawyers, and from colleagues within the organisation. The project team can evolve and review the formal documents covering working practices and what happens in practice. It will encourage and foster greater understanding and teamwork, and ensure that all the parties stay on track in a complex world.

DuPont relationships. If you are using the DuPont Model then the two main key relationship managers can oversee the project team. Further details of the model are set out at Document 3 of Part III – The DuPont Legal Model.

Ensuring attendance. Who is required to attend which management meetings and for what purpose? Are there consequences for non-attendance for busy key lawyers and managers?

Communication

Visit your lawyers. Don't forget to visit the external lawyers' offices from time to time.

Review communication policy and process regularly. Review the actual communication policy and process for strengths and weaknesses, identifying learning points, on an annual basis.

Consider an away day. If you have a large panel, it might be worth considering an annual away day for the teams to meet. See the case study at the end of this chapter and the summary of Carillion's Annual Legal Network Conference in the case study at the end of Chapter 17.

Celebrate success. Publish success stories to all parties to promote best practice.

Methodology, documentation and technology

Tracking methods. Is your tracking to be done electronically, face to face, by telephone or by a mixture of methods? What resources do you require for this?

Use a briefing board. Consider whether an independent extranet briefing board for the panel and your team will be worth the effort or whether you can plug into theirs or they can plug into yours, and on what basis?

Data timing. What data is required on a weekly, monthly, quarterly, and half-yearly or annual basis and for what purpose? Do keep an eye on this as it can grow into a many-headed monster.

Qualitative data. Are you keeping quantitative and qualitative data on performance?

Transaction feedback. A post-transaction feedback questionnaire is invaluable for large or expensive transactions – you may want it to cover most or all of the key performance indicators. See the sample post-transaction questionnaire and drafting notes at Document 16 of Part III.

Management audit. Consider seriously whether an independent management audit can be made by a legal management consultancy on the achievement of key performance indicator(s) and service level agreement data from time to time to ensure objective assessments. If you have Lexcel accreditation you may be able to write your key performance indictor set into your Lexcel manual and audit it as part of your regular assessment.

Updates and changes. If using a small project team, then it may well have responsibility for rolling out updates and changes in the details of all parties, but the key relationship managers should meet at least twice a year for a high-level review of the relationship.

Case study – managing the relationship

Strategic astute planning

Leading the relationship. Right from the start it was essential that Carillion Legal gave a clear lead to the relationship. We were clear that there were huge benefits to be delivered – but equally that they would only be achieved if the process was managed and measured properly. Obviously the relationship would be surrounded with the right words and intent, but this was insufficient – clear leadership was necessary to ensure that the vision and processes were followed and maintained. Our vision included building relationships and delivering promised actions and ensuring that Carillion Legal and our people carried their part of the bargain into effect in full accordance with Carillion's values.

Key performance indicators. Carillion decided that it wanted a mix of measures, and so we used key performance indicators to cover the four key areas of:
- financial
- partnering
- customer service
- business process.

A copy of our key performance indicator set is included at Document 11 of Part III.

We concluded early on that there was no right or wrong key performance indicator set – we developed one we felt appropriate for our business and keep it under review. However, once it existed, we felt we had to continue to run it for a reasonable period – at least a couple of years – to generate information about trends as well as snapshots of performance.

We do this in two ways: a formal key performance indicator set and, as part of that set, an online feedback survey which any user of legal services can access through our intranet. A copy of the feedback survey questionnaire is included at Document 12 of Part III – Carillion online survey feedback questionnaire, and a copy of the report form it generates for each firm on a regular basis is at Document 13 – Network firm half-yearly feedback form. We publish the results twice-yearly to Carillion Legal Network firms and within the business, and provide a formal key performance indicator report twice-yearly which is published within the business.

Stick or carrot? Carillion reviewed internally, and with the Carillion Legal Network firms, whether performance should be rewarded – or punished – directly. We concluded that there should be no direct link since we sought to use the key performance indicator set to improve and change behaviour by encouragement and professionalism rather than punishment, but we keep the position under review.

Business perspective

Review meetings. Where appropriate, we ask our business colleagues to join the reviews, and in some cases we ask them to act as the key contact rather than as a member of Carillion Legal, for instance in relation to property, employment and pensions.

Developing the KPI set. We developed our key performance indicators as a collaborative exercise within the legal team. The necessary data is recorded monthly as part of our normal monthly reporting cycle and formally collated every six months. One of Carillion's values is openness, and as such we publish the key performance data freely both in an interim and year-end report, and on our internal legal intranet which is available in the business.

League tables. Our intranet questionnaire (Document 12 of Part III – Carillion online survey feedback questionnaire) is set up to provide an Excel spreadsheet for each firm (Document 13 – Network firm half-yearly feedback form), and a league table of overall performance. Each firm receives a copy of their own spreadsheet showing their performance in each category against the mean for all firms, and against their performance in the last period. These spreadsheets are then reviewed at each half-yearly review meeting. However, we do not publish the league table outside Carillion Legal – our desire is principally to see continuous improvement in the trends for each firm, rather than necessarily to seek to compare firms whose work is not really comparable in nature.

Clear roles and team working processes

Comparing the in-house and external legal teams. Our key performance set is divided into two parts – one for Carillion Legal itself; one for the Carillion Legal Network. We directly compare the performance of internal and external resource and publish the result.

Half-yearly reviews. Our appraisal systems run as part of the half-yearly review, but we are clear that it is in everyone's interest for us to feed back clearly and honestly on lawyer performance and avoid the danger of falling out with a firm because of one individual performance. We ask the contact partner of each firm, responsible for the client relationship with us, to attend our review meetings. They may bring others – and we may ask them to do so – but the reviews are not intended to require a significant resource.

Continuous improvement. Carillion's culture is about improving performance, not blame, and we have tried to adopt the same approach in our relationship with lawyers. We have the same primary set of law firms on the Network as we did when it was established in 2002 – changes have arisen only due to law firm reorganisation.

Carillion used culture as one of the measures of appointment when we set up the Carillion Legal Network. We feel this meant that we had a head start, in that the selection of firms who we felt could work in accordance with our values meant that we specifically chose firms we thought we could work with.

Carillion's values are central to the way we do business, and are:
- openness
- collaboration
- mutual dependency
- professional delivery
- focus on sustainable, profitable growth
- innovation.

We use tools such as the Carillion Legal Conference and our regular newsletter, as well as secondment and shadowing, to build commonality of understanding.

Our half-yearly management meetings run to a formal agenda, including the identification of new and important issues for the business, trends and forthcoming legislation. We use this review, amongst other things, to prepare training needs analysis.

Communication

Working together. As noted above, we hold two reviews per year with each firm. Carillion's policy is to hold one set of half-yearly reviews at our offices; the other at the office of the law firm concerned – we feel it is important that we are not seen simply to be dragging our Network firms in to see us.

Relationship management. We spread the responsibility internally by appointing an individual lawyer from Carillion Legal to have key responsibility for a Carillon Legal Network firm. This means that no one individual has to spend unreasonable time on managing the relationship. We seek to ensure consistency and the implementation of learning points through the attendance of the Company Secretary and Director of Legal Services at each half-yearly review meeting.

The Network Conference. Carillion holds an annual Carillion Legal Network Conference – we ask representatives of each firm, of the business and members of Carillion Legal to meet. The format varies, but generally includes presentations on our business from executive directors, on the performance of the network and key issues, and a series of workshops on legal or business topics – as well as opportunities to network.

External communication within the Network. Our Network newsletter – Carillion Legal Network News – is used to set out changes, issues and successes across the Network.

Methodology, documentation and technology

Tracking by technology. We began by assuming that what we wanted – and needed – was electronic tracking and reporting. For technical reasons, this was not easily possible and our subsequent reviews have shown that, in our case, we do not feel there would be significant benefit at this stage. It's something we keep under review, though.

Transparency. We keep all our key performance indicator reports available on our intranet site – and use them as part of the twice-yearly review meeting process.

Post-transaction reviews. Carillion sets out to conduct post-transaction reviews for major transactions. We do not use the key performance indicator set to drive these reviews but do carry the work forward into our half-yearly review meetings. A sample post-transaction questionnaire is set out at Document 16 of Part III.

Lexcel accreditation. We have obtained Lexcel accreditation for Carillion Legal – the first in-house corporate team to do so – which will allow a degree of independent audit of Carillion Legal's performance and of the way in which it works with the Network firms.

Key learning points

1. One of the key learning points from our development has been that the choice of key performance indicators is difficult. It is important to have pure financial indicators, but equally important that they are not the only indicator – or even in the majority.

2. Following our recent review of arrangements we have also decided to publish a short handbook setting out basic details for any lawyer who works with us. This will cover areas such as:
   - who we are – people and structure
   - guidelines for working with us – format, communication, emergencies
   - our likes and dislikes
   - billing
   - what happens if it goes wrong.

8   Ending the relationship

INTRODUCTION

Breaking up is hard to do!

That may be a cliché, but one of the hallmarks of a good working relationship is that you will have engineered into it the means and processes to ensure that if you do fall out, you really mean to do so and have established that it is in the mutual interests of the organisation and the law firm to part.

If it does happen, though, you need to be prepared, and in this chapter we look at some of the issues you should think about – and at preparing an exit plan.

Strategic astute plans

Have an exit plan. No really! You would not let your client organisation outsource any other function without one – why do you think you don't need one? See Document 18 of Part III for an example.

Plan for 'why' and 'how'. The exit plan should cover 'why' and 'how' for both sides. Do you know when a law firm can terminate the relationship?

Conflicts of interest. Your plan should include what happens in situations of conflict of interest. Are you aware of the rules? See the relevant Law Society guidelines in Document 17 of Part III. They may mean that law firms are not obliged to be as committed to your cause as you might expect.

Smoothing the process. You might wish to consider a 'sweetener' to smooth this process even if at first consideration this goes against the grain. It may stop undue financial and time delays creeping in and causing frustration to all later.

Business perspective

Discuss with your colleagues. If it really is the end, don't forget to consult your colleagues even if there is no formal process to do so.

Contingency plans are important. Contingency plans to support your business colleagues are required during a break-up. These should cover what support is going to be provided internally or by the new partner, and who is going to project manage the handover.

Clear roles and team working processes

Escalate your dispute – only divorce if you really mean to do so. Your protocol, contract or instruction letter should contain escalation policy and process and a methodology for dealing with complaints – either client related or technically related. There needs to be clarity as to when the business complains direct and when they involve the General Counsel, Head of Legal or Account Manager to fire the bullets. You should also write this into your legal strategy.

Be clear about handover arrangements. Ensure that there is a clear process for handing over to new firms, or your internal legal team, during the termination notice.

Poaching. What prohibitions – if any – are there on poaching individuals from each other's teams?

TUPE. Consider whether there are any Transfer of Undertakings – TUPE – implications of ending particular law firm relationships, especially if you have outsourced lawyers and support staff with the work.

Methodology, documentation and technology

Copyright and IP. You may need to ensure that no copyright infringement takes place, and any software licences are duly executed. You should be clear who owns the copyright to any joint manuals and procedures.

Case study – ending the relationship

Strategic astute plans

The starting point. Carillion started from the premise that we sought long-term relationships with our law firms – but with an expectation that some firms might not wish to work in the way we sought. We have been very pleased to find that each of our chosen firms has, in fact, come up to the mark and we have not had to part company with any of them (other than as a result of firm reorganisation) since setting up the Network in 2002.

Conflict of interest. Our protocols set out what happens in relation to conflict situations – and who firms can work for, with or without consent. We are clear that we do not expect our law firms to act against us, or on the other side of a commercial transaction.

Resolving conflict. We set out to engineer conflict resolution into our protocol arrangements with the member firms of the Carillion Legal Network – we wanted to make it clear that if we and a firm did part company, we were both clear that this was the right thing to do.

Business perspectives

Business issues. We want to find out about issues before they become problems. We do not want either our business colleagues or the law firms to be unhappy about performance or advice without raising those issues – so we consult regularly with our business colleagues to be clear about performance and aim to find out about any concerns, personnel issues and trends before they become a problem.

Clear roles and team working processes

Separation of transactions from management issues. Our processes are clear – any issues are intended to be taken through the legal management route so that the relationship on transactional matters is kept clear of such issues.

Key learning point

In practice, we have had virtually no complaints from within the business during the period since setting up the Network – and we believe this is a testament to the work which we have put into setting up and maintaining the relationships in the first place.

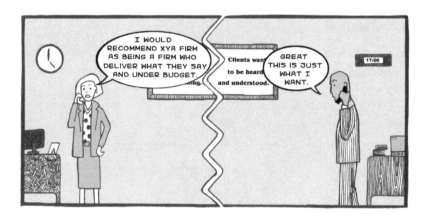

9 International work

INTRODUCTION

Selecting, instructing and managing lawyers internationally are some of the most interesting areas of an in-house lawyer's work. They can also be one of the most risky.

Don't forget that the basic principles we've explored elsewhere in the book apply equally to international instructions.

Strategic astute planning

What do you actually need – one-off advice or long-term arrangements? Do you need one-off advice – say, on an acquisition in a country with which you are unfamiliar, or relatively standard advice on a transaction you do many times across the world?

Are you on the ground already? Do you have a local management presence – even if not an in-house lawyer – and if so are they able to instruct the lawyer on a day-to-day basis?

Role definition. What will your role be?

What do you want from the lawyer? Do you need the lawyer simply to do legal work or to go beyond that, with advice on the business norms of the country, how things are done, translation or other services?

Do you speak the language? If you don't, then you will need to ensure that the lawyer speaks your language. What language do you want to apply to the transaction? If it isn't yours, ensure that translations are accurate – it isn't necessarily reasonable to expect a lawyer to translate complex legal concepts and lengthy drafts into your language.

Culture. Will you be able to do business with the law firm – how does it go about things? Cultural understanding is important.

Business perspective

Follow best practice in selection – regardless of location. Bear in mind the advice on selecting lawyers in Chapters 2 and 3 of this book.

Use other people's experience. Get recommendations – from websites such as Chambers, Legal 500, the International Law Office and the Global Corporate Counsel Association, from other in-house lawyers or from your own external lawyers.

Don't assume you need an international law firm. Don't assume you ought – or ought not – to use the local office of an international law firm. Look at the pros and cons, and what you want them to do. You may find a purely local firm meets your needs better. Either way, bear in mind that you will want to know how things happen in the country, not just the technical legal position.

Visit and meet. If the work you require is at all significant, try to visit in person – meet the lawyers who will do the work, see the office and understand the way they work.

Involve your business colleagues. If your business colleagues will be the main contact day to day, involve them and take them with you.

Ethics and integrity. Take soundings on ethical standards in the country and on the reputation of the law firm. Review available resources for doing business in the country concerned.

Conflicts. Be realistic about conflicts procedures – in some countries you may need to use firms which your competitors also use. If so, ensure you have agreed a conflict procedure with the firm which is sensible and workable.

Define what resource you want – and determine what is available. Identify what resource is available: if you want a firm that is available around the clock, make sure you find one; if you want video conferencing, ensure the firm has it; if you want your lawyers to work during *your* working day, make sure that they will be willing to do so.

Don't assume your usual firm is the right one for an unusual deal. Even if you have a regular firm in a jurisdiction, consider if it is the one for the specific task you have in mind – for instance is the business's day-to-day counsel the right one to do a major corporate restructuring, merger, acquisition or disposal?

Clear roles, team working processes and communication

Related issues. Here issues of roles, team working and communication roll into one.

Check the billing culture locally. Ensure you have clearly understood the financial basis on which the firm will work. Will the firm expect to bill up front? Will it expect a success fee? You may anticipate negotiating fees either before or after the transaction – will the lawyer?

Don't assume everyone understands UK or US billing norms. Do not assume that all will work on the same fee basis as you might expect in the UK. Set out clearly, in writing, how fees will be paid, on what basis, what extras are involved, when bills will be delivered, when you are expected to pay, whether interim billing is required or permitted, and how you will deal with any issues that arise.

Marshal your contact arrangements. Record all the contact details of your chosen lawyer and establish how you wish to communicate with them – if you prefer telephone, be realistic about how this can be achieved if the time zone is very different.

Be clear about reporting. Establish what reporting you require and when – how involved you want to be in the transaction, and what freedom you will give to the lawyer. Be aware that cultural expectations differ significantly – sometimes lawyers will expect to receive very detailed instructions and will not do anything without them; in others they may expect to negotiate and discuss key points which you regard as commercial without involving you at all.

Methodology, documentation and technology

Methods will differ across national boundaries. Consider:

- there may well be a language barrier – even where English is a common language

- the system of law is different – even where it may have a common law basis
- the cultural norms in the country may vary – as may the perceived role of a lawyer
- a transaction you understand fully may be documented wholly differently to the way you expect – for example using much shorter forms than are current in the UK, or by reference to the relevant Civil Code
- there may be timing, registration and regulatory barriers
- the way in which lawyers work – or are perceived – may be very different from the 24/7 resource you are used to in the City or North America.

Write it down. Documenting your requirements may be even more important than in your home jurisdiction – particularly if you are using a firm for the first, and perhaps only, time.

Case study – international work

Strategic astute planning

International strategy. Carillion examines its requirements in each international region, which vary according to specific requirements. Its basic principle is to have a single firm as the key corporate counsel and other firms for particular business requirements – for example, litigation, property and private finance.

Business perspective

Business requirements. In one of its international operations, where it operates largely in joint venture, Carillion uses the legal department of its joint venture partner to provide legal services – an arrangement which works well and to the advantage of both parties. External legal advice is retained only for non-joint venture or for corporate work.

In other territories, work is often required in specific joint ventures for special-purpose companies. In these cases, Carillion may not have a majority holding and it can be tendered for each particular role, often from firms who act for one or other of the partners. In such an instance, a tender arrangement can be helpful and productive.

In each case, it is helpful for the key corporate counsel in each region to have a stable relationship with the business, often becoming a repository of corporate know-how, history and information.

Clear roles, team working processes and communication

Clarity of instructions. It is important for external counsel in international businesses to be clear who is instructing them – particularly if there is no internal lawyer in the relevant business.

Building relationships. Carillion has sought to build relationships with external counsel internationally, for example by inviting them to Carillion's Legal Network Conference, and by copying them with key Carillion documentation and the regular legal network communications.

Methodology, documentation and technology

Proportionality. Carillion reviews in each case what documentation is appropriate and proportionate to our requirements – but we do not use the full United Kingdom protocol for our relationships in international territories. We do, however, use specific written arrangements which are tailored to the business and issues concerned.

Key learning point

One of the key learning points is that in international work more than any other it is necessary to examine one's requirements and identify and instruct against them, without assumptions and presumptions as to the right way of meeting them.

Part II
The techniques

So far this book has concentrated on the process for the delivery of legal services using both external and internal resources. Having decided *what* you want to do, it is now time to review *how* to do it.

This is what separates the excellent game from the game excellent – to move from the performance of one-off excellent activities to a continuous work ethic, values and activities based on excellence as a permanent way of working.

Consistent application of good leadership and management techniques will ensure that you achieve the plans you have to manage, and take not only your external lawyers but your own team with you in providing comprehensive first-class legal support to your organisation.

While some of our tips have been inserted into the relevant chapters in Part I of this book, Part II is meant to be a focus for the important skills set out below:

- **leadership**
- **change management**
- **client relationship management**
- **self-management and development – what's in it for me?**
- **team working for partnering – for both internal and external teams, as well as the joint team created by the two**
- **delegation**
- **appraisal, including feedback**
- **communication skills – giving information**
- **communication skills – receiving information.**

While these skills are necessary in the context of managing external law firms or developing the partnering approach, they are equally relevant in leading and managing internal legal teams, depending on your circumstances.

10 Leadership

INTRODUCTION

Without effective leadership your plans have little chance of success.

The primary force behind change of any significance is leadership not management – effective leadership produces useful change. To maximise the effective use of external resources with your own internal ones, you will need to be able to live your vision.

Do you remember the words from the Preface? There are three kinds of legal departments:

- those that make things happen
- those that watch what happens
- and those that wonder what's happening.

Leadership, here, is about leading constructive change in the provision of legal services by setting the direction of the new way of working with external lawyers, aligning everyone involved to it, and achieving your vision by motivating and inspiring the lawyers and business colleagues. Without appropriate and sufficient leadership, the probability of mistakes increases greatly and the probability of success decreases accordingly.

If you are a sole in-house lawyer you will still want to lead the external resource rather than be led by it.

Leadership techniques

Identify the external environment. Look again at the tools outlined in Section 1 of Chapter 1 – they will help you to understand your environment to identify the key themes for managing your external lawyers. Effective leaders are very good at assessing the political, social and technological arenas in order to choose their vision of the future.

Practise creative thinking. Think creatively – openly, without barriers and towards your desired solutions – working first in routine processes before moving to non-routine situations and assessing your ability to influence the actions, beliefs and feelings of other lawyers to support any change management projects you have initiated for your department.

Encourage forward thinking in your team. A good leader will also encourage all members of any internal team to be aware of changes that are happening in your sector and the profession, and look out for the ones coming down the track. Don't forget to reward this with recognition – particularly if your team does not currently do this.

Articulate your vision. Tell everyone what you want to achieve and what it looks like, including the criteria for success which you should have developed by using the tips in Chapter 5 – Leveraging value out of legal costs. The vision is your platform to lead others – you can't lead without one. Leaders need to be able to visualise results.

Walk the talk. Show the way by 'walking the talk'. This is the most critical success factor in aligning lawyers and business colleagues to your vision, in combination with a consistency of approach. You must act and behave fully in accordance with your vision. Any indication that your public face is only for public consumption will bring down your vision – you will lose face and confidence with both internal and external teams. This factor comes up time and time again as being the key thing that will destroy the vision and the team's effectiveness or performance.

Understand and align your values. Don't forget to understand and align the values of your organisation and your internal and external teams. Stephen Mayson in his book *Making Sense of Law Firms* states that 'the challenge is balancing client satisfaction, internal and external lawyer satisfaction while remaining true to everyone's values and beliefs'. Values and beliefs propel lawyers into action. It is essential to engage hearts and minds to produce effective change.

Encourage and praise. Use acknowledgement and praise to practise encouragement of your external and internal teams – they must believe in the possibility and actuality of change, and will go that extra mile to achieve your vision.

Understand the components of leadership. If you are unclear as to what the components of leadership look like, see the leadership competency section 2

74

in Document 2 – Competencies for in-house lawyers. The competencies of leadership are vital, so we set them out in full below:

- demonstrate commitment to the organisation's aims, values and strategy
- use oral and written influencing skills
- provide motivation
- generate and encourage creative solutions to problems
- focus on results
- anticipate, facilitate and/or lead change
- deal flexibly and confidently with the unexpected
- adapt behaviour and style to the situation and competence of individuals
- create and convey a clear vision of success.

This is a good base from which to ascertain whether you want to widen the contents or change these for your organisation. Review against your own skill set using a scoring system of 1–5 for each part to determine where you should focus your leadership development and practice.

Leadership cannot be understood in the abstract and needs to be experienced in real life. Be aware that these skills are like your sporting or other skills – you will not become an expert overnight. It will take practice.

Learn from others. If you know you're not good at a particular skill, find someone who is good at that particular skill. This is what brilliant leaders do – they know how to harness the skills of others for their team and organisation.

Change your leadership style as your teams develop. Be aware that, as you move through your change process, your levels of control over your lawyers should loosen and adjust as you empower your lawyers to build their skills, experience and alignment to your vision, and to innovate.

Change your leadership style as your role changes. Leadership does not just happen when you reach the top. The nature of leadership will be different when you are leading a team and when you lead a full department. Practise your leadership skills in leading a transaction in preparation for moving into a more challenging leadership role.

Review your personal leadership. You can lead at any time in your career in three distinct areas:

- your personal centre of technical excellence
- your people skills
- your own positive values (e.g. sincerity) and integrity, establishing your reputational capital for when you reach the top. This is a powerful leadership skill, and it is never too early to start with this one.

Remember leaders need help too. External support for potential leaders is available from a number of sources:

- There are a number of consultancies offering leadership support and coaching; some have specific knowledge of lawyers and the legal sector and others do not. In fact many leaders have some form of coaching support as a matter of course.
- Leadership training is available from a number of legal and non-legal providers.
- A client development centre set up by a national law firm works with various legal departments on leadership as a client service. Your own external law firms may offer a similar service.

11 Change management

INTRODUCTION

Invariably, using external lawyers to provide legal services creates change within your organisation and a section on change management techniques is essential. This chapter should be read to support Chapter 3 – Procurement, Chapter 4 – Panel reviews, and Chapter 6 – Beginning the relationship, of Part I of this book.

> 'It should be considered that there is nothing more difficult to handle, more doubtful of success or more dangerous to carry through than to initiate new order of things'.
>
> Machiavelli, *The Prince*

Please examine carefully the 'Human resistance to change' graph on page 79. This shows how people find it difficult to accept change. In some organisations, there is so much change that many people never get past the stage of confusion. Is that where you want your team, your partners or yourself to be? If not, you must manage and lead appropriate and constructive change.

Techniques

Assess your data. Take time out to assess the data and your earlier decisions to consider their potential impact on your change process. This assessment will provide you with some ideas for the planning of the transition and achieving the vision you are aiming for with your external lawyers. You should do this whether or not you aim for a partnering approach. Some project managers believe that planning should take 20 per cent of the time spent on any change management arrangements.

Involve everyone. Where possible, involve everyone in the change process and methodology – being part of the process gives everyone a sense of ownership and belonging. Bring your team – which should include your external law firm or firms – together to start the planning process for the change you wish to effect. Educating and involving your external law firms at an early stage can be very helpful – before you negotiate or impose the new regime on them. Imposing anything on anyone creates resentment and inhibits best performance – consider how you react if you're told something is a done deal.

Prepare contingency plans. Don't forget to include contingency plans to anticipate and cope with the unforeseen and any setbacks and delays in implementation.

Prepare communication plans. Ensure that there is an effective communication policy and process, and that they are implemented to head off the issues which might lead to confusion and dissent in the teams. Producing and dealing with damage limitation communications can require far more effort and time than the resource required to get it right first time through your official channels.

Use surveys and focus groups. Consider conducting surveys, climate reviews and focus groups to collect both quantitative and qualitative data at the start of and during significant milestones. You can also use them periodically – say once or twice a year. They will give you an early indication of how well things are progressing – or whether you have a specific problem that you need to head off early.

Use the right leader. If you are not leading the change team then put a respected person in charge of the process or transition team to ensure that the change process has the credibility to achieve your vision. Focus your efforts on being visible to support that person and team where it counts.

Train and develop your teams in the new methods. Provide training for both internal and external lawyers on the new methods, and in the values you want to inculcate in the new team. Training itself is a group activity which will assist in building teams that function well together.

Consider using help! Consider bringing in outside help such as coaches or internal or external consultants, either for the whole or part of the process. If you do this, you must retain responsibility and visibility – and be seen to do so.

Celebrate and reward success. Establish new symbols of change and celebratory events for achieving significant milestones.

Recognise achievements. Provide recognition for law firms for the challenges overcome as well as the achievements as you move to the new order. Try to provide this recognition in some tangible way – for example, lunch with the key business people within your organisation for their particular type of work.

Understand that change takes time. Change has an element of discomfort for us all and the inevitable resistance to it has to be managed. Identify the position of any team or individual lawyer on the graph below to choose the appropriate method of proceeding as quickly as possible through the various stages of resistance to the ultimate goal of problem solving. The common factors which assist this process are education, communication and involvement – but some emotional support will almost certainly also be required. Coaching and mentoring can be particularly effective here in assisting lawyers to come to terms with change.

Human resistance to change

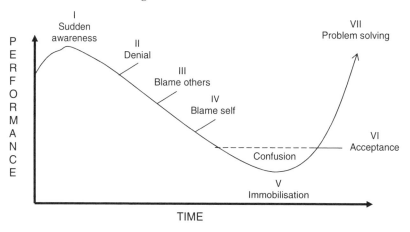

Source: *Death and Dying* by Elisabeth Kubler-Ross, 1969. Reproduced with permission.

Take the pulse. As you roll out your change process, make time to 'take the pulse' of the changes being experienced periodically. You need to ensure that you continue to have buy-in from the main stakeholders in the process.

Implement and track progress. Implement the new methods and track their impact with the external law firms to create a culture of continuous improvement and an ethos of working which avoids ineffective methods becoming embedded.

12 Client relationship management

Client relationship management is critical for both the internal and external team. It should be seamless between the two, but is the principal responsibility of the General Counsel and his or her internal lawyers and legal managers. They must set the tone and direction for the external law firms.

There are many theories of client relationship management but the two books the authors found particularly useful are *Head2Head* by Paul Gilbert and *The Trusted Advisor* by David Maister, Charles Green and Robert Galford.

Techniques

Share your vision. It is imperative that your organisation can see *and share* your vision, your leadership and integrity, and your management and team working skills as well as the value you bring to the organisation. If communication fails here, it is down to you. See also Chapter 17 – Communication skills.

Listen. You need to listen. No really! Then you need to act in ways that show the organisation that you are aware of its underlying needs and not just acting on the overt request for legal service. One of the critical listening techniques is to reflect back to the individual business representatives of your organisation what you have heard in their own language.

Understand what your organisation values. In his book *Head2Head*, Paul Gilbert sets out what clients value – and argues that, generally, it is how things are done, rather than simply what those things are. We set out below some of the factors identified. He suggests that clients generally value those factors set out in italics more than the in other factors – but that does not mean that you can ignore the other factors. They are taken as a given, and you must have those skills before you can develop the client-focused skills. What makes you appear to excel and be more attractive to the client – and that includes your organisation – is being good at those in italics:

- *people skills*/legal skills
- *speed of response*/accuracy of response
- *helpfulness*/the right answer
- *work beyond the brief*/work within the brief
- *build relationships*/be reactive
- *team player*/impartial neutral
- *creative*/secure
- *ensuring the business is successful*/ensuring the business is protected
- *delivery*/content.

This is because clients can understand and evaluate the soft factors more effectively than they can evaluate the legal services being provided.

Carry out client surveys. An important system for listening is the use of client surveys – especially if you show that you act on the feedback, and the next steps are fed into the performance management systems operated by the law firm and in-house legal function. See, for example, Document 12 – Carillion online survey feedback questionnaire.

Use single-point post-transaction reviews. As a supplement to your formal feedback system, or if you prefer not to use systematic processes, at the end of each transaction ask individual business colleagues within your organisation for one improvement suggestion. This should be one improvement you and your external lawyers can make to continue to improve the service that you provide. It should go without saying that you need to listen and act upon the suggestion.

Recognise success. Do you have a recognition system for when the teams do well? This is particularly helpful if it is a joint system. If the rewards are social activities they may also deepen team knowledge and promote effective working – but be sure that such activities do not overstep the bounds of proper procurement or suggest that you are receiving inappropriate hospitality from your law firms.

Understand client relationship competencies. The client relationship competencies set out in Document 2 of Part III – Competencies for in-house lawyers' – articulates the constituent parts of successful client relationship management skills. Review your own skills, and those of your internal and external teams, against them and work on areas for improvement:

- promote the legal department to the widest possible internal client base
- establish and agree corporate client requirements
- manage corporate clients' needs and expectations
- meet corporate client requirements
- enable managers to recognise the need for in-house legal services
- enable managers to identify and minimise legal risks
- contribute to crisis management in the organisation
- develop and implement quality assurance
- manage complaints
- manage relationships with regulators.

Aim to be a Trusted Adviser. There are different types of relationships with clients but the most coveted is that of 'Trusted Adviser'. Do read about the evolution of the client–adviser relationship, which is considered in depth in the book *The Trusted Advisor* by David Maister, Charles Green and Robert Galford. Extracted below is their view of the evolution of the role of Trusted Adviser with some examples:

First Step	Subject Matter (*employment legislation*) or Process Expert (*employment tribunal*)
Second Step	Subject Matter Expert plus Affiliated Field – *now includes directors and senior management responsibilities*
Third Step	Valuable Resource – understands your business and the context in which you operate, and has exceeded your expectations in Steps 1 and 2 – *now incorporates commercial and sector information/ experience within the advice*
Fourth Step	Trusted Advisor – having provided advice proactively *you are now becoming the first person the client turns to about both personal and professional issues which are open to discussion and debate, and for strategic second opinions*

The first type of relationship is based around a service offering, the second is based on needs and it only becomes relationship-based in the third step. The last one is obviously based on trust. If you are really serious about excelling at client relationship management then this book is a must for you.

Consider the DuPont Model. As we have said, the DuPont Model is well established and may well have elements that you will wish to consider. See Document 3 of Part III – the DuPont Legal Model.

13 Self-management and development

INTRODUCTION

As a good leader, you will want to show initiative on self-management and development that will allow you to lead and manage your external resources.

You might want to consider writing down your own experiences, especially if you are making real and sustained changes to the way you select and manage external lawyers. Prepare a folder defining your own learning and success. Life is constantly evolving at work and it is easy to take for granted that you are enhancing your own skills and experience.

Your 'success' folder should contain what worked and what didn't. This will give you an easy reference point for the next time you embark on a major change to your panel or restructuring the services, e.g. outsourcing to private practice. You never know when you might want to write your own book and the source material will be readily to hand!

You will also require your external lawyers to continually develop their interpersonal skills, so look for synergies and joint opportunities for learning – see the case study in Chapter 17 which covers Carillion's Service and Communication Conference 2006.

Techniques for self assessment

Review your own role. Before looking at what you want to outsource, you may want to review the role of General Counsel, Head of Legal or Legal Director or Company Secretary. Does the organisation see your primary role as cost saving or process improvement or service function? Build in some thinking and strategic time on the different roles of the in-house lawyer – see Document 1 of Part III – The role of in-house lawyers – model of multi hats of in-house lawyers.

Compare the roles described in Document 1 with your own situation to establish if you are fulfilling your potential in your current role or whether you could expand or remould your role to suit your capabilities and potential.

Review your legacy. Are you planning your own career within and outside the organisation – if you're not, who is? Another way to view this is to ask – 'what is your legacy to the organisation going to be?'.

Develop your self-awareness techniques. Self-awareness should not be underrated as a skill. Do you know your own strengths and areas for improvement? If you do not, others will! You should review your strengths and areas of improvement on a yearly basis. If your organisation does not provide a framework to do so, see the Personal assessment form at Exercise 4 of Part III.

Audit your skills. Exercise 4 of Part III – Personal assessment – can also be used to conduct a specific audit of your skills for managing and motivating external lawyers. You might want to understand your current capabilities for this role as well as what you need to develop to shine in this management position.

Benchmark yourself. The self-management competency on page 130 (Document 2 of Part III – Competencies for in-house lawyers) can also be used to benchmark yourself. How well do you score?
- Manage conflict demands and priorities
- Demonstrate consistency and sound reasoning in decision making – even when under pressure
- Act assertively
- Behave ethically and display integrity
- Actively seek and create challenging opportunities for self-development
- Participate in team working
- Learn to build your own strengths and recognise and seek to improve weaknesses
- Keep abreast of key developments in law and legal practice
- Be open to change
- Be aware of and able to confront your own prejudices
- Work within equalities policy and good-practice guidelines.

Self-development techniques

Prepare a self-development plan and use help. Undertake your self-development plan with one or more of the following to help you:

- a coach, either internally within your organisation or externally. The coach will assist you to find your own motivation and solutions as well as keeping you on track. Coaches are used both by law firms and organisations
- a mentor, either a senior person within the organisation, or your law firms or somebody you admire outside this circle, who can pass on the benefit of their experiences to you
- your manager.

Networking. Networking can also be used as a learning experience, especially in your own sector – such as the Commerce and Industry Group. See list of networking groups at page 174.

Further reading. Reading appropriate leadership and management books, then sharing debating and **practising** what you have learned is a useful tool for self-development. Please see Further reading and resources at the end of this book.

Professional development. Undertaking part-time degree or professional courses on the subject of your choice, MBA or Business School learning, or attending appropriate courses on leadership and management either within the organisation or outside can be helpful – internal courses can build your credibility and relationships within the organisation; external ones can give you a broader perspective.

People watching. Use meetings as a way to observe good communication styles – what is effective and what is not. Use role models as well – and observe them too.

Presentations. Presentations can also be a self-development tool – especially in the early stages addressing one's own team and learning from feedback, before you are asked to present to the Board or to 500 people after dinner!

Back to the floor. Ask for a role swap or secondment into another department in your organisation or onto a major project. This will allow you to see what skills you have which are transferable to new roles.

Benchmarking. Compare your performance to outside parameters to learn from the differences and build a portfolio of data for quality improvement initiatives.

Build a skills ladder. Does your department or organisation have training 'ladders' showing the 'how' training or competency profile required for different stages of the lawyer's role or career? Do your external lawyers? If not, you could work on one together, or buy in an external consultant to assist in tailoring one for your circumstances.

The review loop. You must practise and honestly assess what works for you and what does not, then refine your techniques and then go on to more practice. One definition of madness is 'doing the same thing over and over again and expecting different results'.

Don't be afraid of failure. Last, but not least, don't be afraid of mistakes or crushed by them; they are signposts that you are really being stretched and challenged. Constant practice will see continuous improvement in your leadership and management skills.

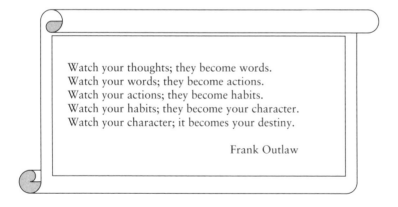

> Watch your thoughts; they become words.
> Watch your words; they become actions.
> Watch your actions; they become habits.
> Watch your habits; they become your character.
> Watch your character; it becomes your destiny.
>
> Frank Outlaw

14 Team working for partnering

INTRODUCTION

You should be planning for:

- the long-term legal strategy for your organisation
- the operational support required to implement it
- the internal and external structures you need now and in the future.

If you are not carrying out this planning, who is?

If you want to develop the partnering approach – such as that used by Carillion – then team management skills are essential. These skills will enable the seamless delivery of the first-class commercial legal services by you, your internal team and the external law firms.

To help you achieve a very close working partnering relationship, this section looks at:

- building teams
- managing teams
- developing teams.

Appraising and feedback are also critical to success. These are covered in detail in Chapter 16.

Techniques for building a 'partnering' team

The lawyer as leader. So let's start with the leader. Do you understand how teams are built? If not, does your own organisation have any training or methodology or role models for you to adopt – or do you need to go outside the organisation to find them? There are many to choose from – some are mentioned in Further reading and resources at the end of this book.

Use your organisation's training provision. Go on relevant partnering or team building training provided by your organisation to ensure that your team building activities and methodology used are in line with the ones used by your colleagues.

Inclusion or induction. The first step in building any team is around settling in the new members and working practices. You need to build in team events and practices that encourage people to get to know each other and feel that they belong together as a team.

Most people will naturally want to conform – even lawyers – and so will look to the designated leader for acceptance and guidance. Some authors refer to this initial stage as 'inclusion' or 'norming'. Maslow, in his book *Motivation and Personality*, felt that there was a hierarchy of needs from the lowest to the highest level of complexity, comprising those of:

- physiological
- safety
- belonging
- esteem
- self-actualisation.

This inclusion or induction phase fulfils the 'belonging' need in Maslow's hierarchy. Please see Further reading and resources.

Meet early, meet often. Where possible 'meeting and greeting' events should take place prior to working together on the 'burning the midnight oil' transactions.

Value the home team. Always ensure that your internal team feels valued. The perception that external resourcing is somehow better is easy to establish and hard to dispel.

Include the external team. If you are aiming for the partnering approach, it is vital that your external lawyers are included in the team building meetings and events. Where possible, it is also a good idea to include them in the team building exercises that you arrange for your own team to build and cement relationships at all levels. The number of people involved may make this impractical as a complete group – but you might well be able to welcome secondees to your meetings and events, so building relationships over time.

Build the relationship through away days or conferences. You can set up away days or conferences which include the business, the internal and external teams as participants – see Case Study to Part II, on Carillion's Legal Network Conference on Service and Communication. However, it is vital that these events have clear objectives and a purpose – everyone present must expect to get something out of them. They may work on several levels – telling people about the organisation, allowing networking opportunities, learning about processes and procedures, and developing skills.

Manage changes within the team. Don't forget to have an 'inclusion' process to manage changes to the current team of lawyers. You might use a buddy system to speed up integration.

Set your standards from the start. From the beginning, set high standards and positive values for the whole team. In the book *Explore Your Values*, Professor Honey describes twelve value exercises for teams to complete to align their values and identify differences. Using such exercises will enable teams to widen their knowledge of themselves and each other and become effective together. Please see Further reading and resources.

Celebrate diversity. Last, but not least, is your team diverse? Diversity means many things – male/female, tall/short, black/white, able/disabled, representatives from the different cultures in the make-up of your own organisation – which should allow you to achieve the best from everyone within your internal and external teams. In the legal context, lawyers from diverse backgrounds are happier and more productive if they are appreciated and included rather than simply assimilated or tolerated. Your organisation may well have a diversity policy and compulsory diversity training to ensure you achieve the best in recruitment, development and retention in your team. Some in-house lawyers are insisting on knowing the diversity policies and mix of their external lawyers. Are you?

Techniques for managing the 'partnering' team

Capturing the spirit. The second stage of team building is reached when the lawyers feel that they have 'got the measure' of their fellow lawyers and have benchmarked themselves against each other. Lawyers will now be competing with each other and demonstrating their own significance within the team. The challenge at this stage is to capture the team spirit and energy – and ensure it is directed externally to benefit the team, rather than internally so that it creates unease and distrust.

This stage is often called the assertion or 'storming' stage and needs to be managed with a firm hand – but also with awareness that too much control will stifle innovation and high performance. In Maslow's hierarchy of needs, this stage demonstrates both self-esteem and esteem from others.

Managing with the common goal in mind. To manage the partnering team effectively, you need to be:

- providing clarity about the common goal or goals, to ensure that everyone in the team understands what they are
- mindful that such management means getting things done through the lawyers – they are your driving force for excellence
- encouraging individual lawyers to raise their differing viewpoints whilst at the same time ensuring that they accept collective responsibility for joint decisions and actions
- able to ensure that joint efforts are co-ordinated and rewarded, for example through bonuses that take account of individual and team success
- able to ensure that management systems and procedures take account of your organisation's business and legal objectives
- continuously seeking to implement ways of providing improved quality
- providing the lawyers with sufficient financial information so that the financial targets are met.

Mindful of the key competencies in managing your external lawyers. The general framework set out in Document 2 of Part III – Competencies for in-house lawyers – is worth keeping in mind:

- develop productive working relationships
- brief external lawyers and others
- enable external service providers to understand the internal corporate procedures
- establish and agree your requirements with external lawyers and others
- supervise and review progress and ensure your agreed outcomes are achieved
- manage costs
- manage potential conflicts of interest
- identify appropriate providers of external legal and other services, ensuring best value.

Mindful of the key competencies in managing individuals and teams.
Additionally, you should focus on the competencies also referred to in
Document 2:

- contribute to the recruitment and selection of personnel
- plan, allocate and evaluate the work of teams and individuals
- promote team working
- contribute to the learning and development of teams and individuals
- assess and provide feedback to teams and individuals on their performance
- empower teams and individuals
- delegate work to others
- support individuals who have problems affecting their performance
- deal positively and objectively with conflict
- manage change.

Develop your networking activities. Continue to encourage both formal
and informal networking activities between internal and external lawyers
to give opportunities for everyone to meet in a variety of situations.
An intranet bulletin board can also be effective to facilitate such
information – as can an external newssheet from your team to your
external lawyers.

Secondments. Arrange for secondments (with full debriefing on completion
to their manager and team) as a way of increasing the knowledge and
effectiveness between teams of the different patterns of working and
stresses. This can be effective both between different parts of your internal
team and between internal and external legal teams.

**Use meetings as a way to observe communication styles – what is working
and what is not.** You may even want to designate an individual to observe
and then share their observations with the group, and/or rotate the chair of
the meeting around the room. There is nothing more powerful than standing
in someone's shoes to understand what is or is not possible.

Review what's going on. Arrange for surveys on what is working well and
the inhibitors to working well for completion by both the internal and
external teams on an anonymous basis if objective data is required. These
surveys can replace or supplement the transactional and/or yearly feedback
depending on your own preferences.

Analyse material mistakes. Have a framework for analysing 'mistakes' of a certain value or importance to ensure that these can be corrected when they arise and process and systems are reviewed. Be clear that there are risks and that you are not seen to be looking for scapegoats or someone to blame – it is important to establish from the outset that you are aiming to improve, not simply looking for someone to fire.

Understand cultural differences. As many legal teams work within global organisations, and so global cultures and diverse team members provide a variety of approaches and perspectives to give your team an opportunity to be ahead of the game. The extent to which you pull together the attitudes and beliefs, values and behaviour, and management practices and polices within an organisation determines the level to which you manage diversity effectively. Time has to be spent discovering the differences to maximise the benefits and allow them to be shared. Workshops based around the sharing and discussion of values can promote good team spirit and working practices.

Techniques for developing the 'partnering' team

Performing. The next stage is reached when all your team members are directed to the common goal of the team and everyone is pulling in the same direction. This is often referred to either as the co-operation or 'performing' stage. It represents the 'self-actualising' stage of Maslow's hierarchy of needs.

Devise team development plans. Ask the team to devise development plans for the partnering teams. You and the team need to plan the work and allocate it amongst the team, setting individual objectives and providing feedback on relationships. In dealing with problems you must be careful to be fair and even-handed in all your dealings. This should be done in conjunction with the external law firms so that all lawyers are being developed to a common goal or goals.

Know when you've arrived. You will know when you have reached the stage of the developed team, since high performance and innovative teams have a number of hallmarks, such as:
- trust
- autonomy

- integrity
- authenticity
- passion for the success of the group
- enthusiasm for the common tasks and continuous improvements
- support for all members
- initiative
- security within the group.

Communicate success. If you have an intranet that is accessible and used by all, then using a bulletin board approach to post lessons learned can be very helpful. If not, then these learning points can either be covered in a newsletter or by email or in the feedback at the end of a major transaction.

Further development techniques. As well as some of the techniques set out in the above section on managing teams, some of the following may be considered:

- Role enlargement – three stages – first, participating in a due diligence process; second, managing a project under supervision; and, third, leading one.
- Role shadowing – allowing lawyers of the organisation to shadow partners in law firms and vice versa.
- Role rotation – swapping roles to multi-skill the lawyers, e.g. moving to an equivalent role in another team in the department; working in another business in the group.
- Project management roles – having responsibility of process improvements between the businesses, internal and external lawyers.

Compare the firms – and your own team. Benchmarking the law firms if you use more than one with each other and/or your own team. See, for example, the Carillion online survey feedback questionnaire and feedback report form in Part III at Documents 12 – Carillion online survey feedback questionnaire, and 13 – Network firm half-yearly feedback form, respectively.

Use meetings. Use meetings as development and learning experiences:

- rotate the chair
- rotate responsibility for setting them up and determining the format
- rotate other roles as appropriate.

15 Delegation

INTRODUCTION

If you do not delegate, then your new partnering approach or working practices for your internal and external lawyers will fail.

Delegation is an essential skill for anyone managing an in-house legal function, because you have a job that cannot be accomplished alone, nor solely with an internal team. The following techniques can also be used for your internal team. As a manager you will be more proficient at many tasks than your staff – and unless you delegate this will remain the case. The desire to be in total control is an essential human trait – and very common in those who choose to become lawyers. But it is impossible in business – the key message here is that you need to target control of the process, not the person.

Techniques

Be clear what you are delegating from the outset. Clarity of what you want to be done and achieved, communicated well, will ensure your delegation is effective. You should only change what you are delegating when it is really important – be careful not to undermine the responsibility you have delegated.

Let your lawyers help you to shine in the eyes of your organisation. If you enlist skilled and motivated law firms to carry out the delegated task or transaction, and they do so well, in accordance with the goals and objectives you have set, and achieve the task on time and budget, this will enhance your reputation as a leader and manager internally. You can concentrate on the key tasks – delegating those which are better done by others. The key task here might be management of internal and external politics to ensure everyone understands who is doing what, and why.

Manage your time. If possible only attend meetings directly relevant to the achievement of your overall vision and goals for partnering with your external lawyers, unless you are actually leading a high profile transaction for your organisation with the firm. Do not simply duplicate your role or the role of the external lawyers – you should each be doing different things.

Understand why you are delegating. Understand why you are delegating to a particular team (internal or external). Obviously, matching the lawyer or law firm to the task is crucial to success and this information should allow you to assess and define the law firm's fitness for your purpose.

Don't just delegate the jobs you don't like or find difficult – people will know. This will destroy the building of credibility and trust in you and the external lawyers.

Be S.M.A.R.T. Use the S.M.A.R.T. test for ensuring your instructions and objectives for any delegated tasks and transactions are clear:
- Specific
- Measurable
- Agreed
- Realistic
- Time-phased.

Generate continuous improvement. Give a reward or prize for the lawyer who comes up with the best workable ideas for the team on a monthly basis or at the end of each transaction – make a habit of challenging into a long-standing routine. Your organisation will not stand still: neither should you.

Be consistent in your external instructions. When briefing your external law firm ensure that you adopt a consistent approach.
- *Checklist*. You should use a checklist to avoid omissions and overlaps in oral or written instructions.
- *Aims and objectives*. Ensure that each law firm is fully aware of the organisation's, the department's and the specific team's aims and objectives, as well as the essentials for the specific transaction or activity being delegated.
- *Organisational processes*. Any organisational processes you have that will impact on the transaction or project being delegated should be used and appreciated in the context of the briefing and or the transaction being delegated. These may include risk management, corporate governance, money laundering policy,

Total Quality Management policies and Client Relationship Management programmes.

- *Authority levels*. The external law firm must understand how much overt or implied authority it has without referring back to you – this may be verbal or written or both. A dialogue will be necessary to ensure you both have the same understanding. You must avoid unexpected surprises caused by a failure to recognise authority levels or an understanding of when they must hold the corporate line.
- *Adequate resources*. Everyone must have the resources they need or know where to get them to complete the task(s) and/or transaction(s).
- *Clear time-scales*. All the time-scales must be articulated and not guessed at – they must be planned for. You should all understand which time-scales are critical and which may contain a degree of flexibility – for example, completing or signing transactions before year-end or accounting deadlines, or so that announcements can be co-ordinated with business goals.
- *Problem handling*. Ensure that there are clear processes for raising difficult issues, handling mistakes by the external law firm, disagreements about how things are done and the consequences of going against the team in place before such issues arise. You may wish to ensure that you comply with a formal instruction protocol – see, for example, Carillion's Draft Relationship Protocol at Document 9 and Working Instructions Checklist at Document 10 of Part III.
- *Joint brief*. The external law firms are allowed to contribute to and comment on the brief in their own words to ensure that everyone understands it fully.

Use appropriate monitoring methods – for transactions. Monitoring methods for consideration when managing delegated *transactions* to external lawyers include the following:

- *Meetings*. What type of meetings do you require, if you require any at all? Are any business ones required for this delegated transaction? What should be their frequency, and with whom?
- *Task and activity lists*. If you want your external lawyers to use task and activity schedules of any type, then lead the way.

- *Monthly written reporting.* You may wish to use a formal, detailed format to ensure that you capture all the information you need, and do so in a consistent format to allow ease of reference and reading.
- *Exceptional reports.* If you think that these will be useful then agree at the outset what areas they should cover. Then review their use at the end of the transaction so you keep the ones that worked and delete the ones that did not.
- *Risk management reports.* Do you have specific requirements for this type of transaction? You may well require the completion of a detailed risk matrix or profile to track compliance on a regular basis through the transaction.
- *Contingency plan tracking.* This may be required depending on the risk profile of the activity.
- *Computer monitoring system.* Use the tracking systems of any case management or computer reporting system you have.
- *Appraisal and review.* What system will you use to appraise how well the external law firm performed, the task done, the desired outcome achieved, what the team member learned and so on? If you agree the review process in the beginning, you increase its effectiveness and do not end up imposing one at the end in a potentially emotional scenario.
- *Coaching systems.* These will build up the expertise of the internal and external teams – so you both can shine.

Use appropriate monitoring methods – for tasks. Monitoring methods for consideration when managing specific delegated *tasks* to external lawyers include the following.

- *Involvement in correspondence.* Do you want to control sign-off, or give second opinions from a mentoring point of view, or coach the team member to find the improvements themselves? Be clear from the outset what is required.
- *Reports.* Will you require short written reports about their actions, results, or learning points? If your organisation has these in template form, you can ask the external lawyer to write these up in their own words if this would be useful when appraising the work by you and the lawyer concerned. Don't forget to include a discussion around

what changes on both sides may need to be made to improve performance.

- *Prioritise availability*. How many times is a transaction held up because you are too busy? What does this say to your clients, and your team? If you cannot fix a meeting for weeks, you may not be delegating enough.
- *Consistency*. Last, but not least – be consistent.

Choose what you think will work for you and track its effectiveness for you and the external lawyers. One size doesn't fit all – and you shouldn't be using every technique every time.

16 Appraisals and feedback

INTRODUCTION

The ability to provide effective appraisals with beneficial feedback is so critical for you to be in the 'game excellence' box rather than the 'excellent game' that it deserves a section of its own with a 'game plan' for you to follow.

Feedback enables individuals and teams to have a better understanding of their individual and collective contributions. It is an excellent tool to provide recognition of what is working well. This in turn encourages the positive and forward-looking working practices and behaviours you want to see. Feedback should be used as a dialogue – not a one-way conversation.

These techniques can be used for your internal team as well as your external lawyers – but remember, many organisations will have their own methodology; do ensure that you use it effectively.

Techniques for giving feedback to external law firms and lawyers

Preparation. Before giving any feedback, ask yourself the following questions:

- *Why are you saying this?* Is it for the recipient's benefit or yours? Ideally, in a feedback session, it should be only for the benefit of the recipient.
- *What are you trying to achieve?* Do you have development goals in mind? Try to relate the feedback to individual personal development plans.
- *Are you in a sufficiently private space?* If not, wait until you are.
- *Have you done enough preparation?* Do you have enough examples to provide a base for discussion – especially if the appraisal session is a formal transactional or periodic appraisal? Ask the law firm to do preparation too – and to bring their examples along. Without

examples of the behaviour you wish to applaud or to change, the session is simply a giving of opinions, not one of useful feedback.

- *Have you got a checklist?* This can provide a useful aide-mémoire for the session. Don't use it as a script, though.
- *How can you say what you want to say skilfully and assertively?* Have a few phrases ready to use and practise these with a 'buddy' for feedback on their impact. You need to ensure that feedback will be received in the spirit it is intended. We influence others by *how* we deliver the feedback as well as through *what* we say.
- *Do you know the communication style of the recipient?* If so can you accommodate that in the feedback? See the case study which outlines Carillion's Communication and Service Conference at the end of Chapter 17 – Communication skills.
- *Are you fully aware of your own communication style?* This includes the impact of your body language and choice of language. For example, is your body language relaxed or are you tense and tired after a long day? Would it be better to postpone the conversation until you are more relaxed?

During the session. In the one-to-one feedback session, focus on the following issues. These issues apply whether it is a formal or transactional session.

- *Atmosphere.* Try to create an informal and unhurried atmosphere to encourage an open discussion and give time for the recipient to open up.
- *Performance outcomes.* Consider the outcome of the performance which is under review. *Always separate the behaviour from the personalities.* You are entitled – and indeed should be encouraged – to comment on behaviour, but you should not make this a personal judgement about an individual lawyer. This does not mean you cannot feed back to the law firm that the chemistry is not working – that is important and key to the relationship. It is entirely reasonable to ask that firms change lawyers who do not build a satisfactory chemistry with you and your team.
- *Specific rather than general* issues. If you focus on specific examples, the law firm and its lawyer can understand their own formulae for success and replicate them for you. If you do make a general observation, follow up with a specific example.

- *Observation rather than judgements.* What you saw or heard them *say* is vital – not simply the meaning you ascribed to the action. For example, saying 'I saw your lawyer looking through your papers or using your Blackberry for five minutes when I was in the middle of my presentation' is powerful. 'You had no intention of listening to me' is not.
- *Use descriptions.* You should always use descriptions as a base for the discussions rather than judgements which can create defensive behaviours. Describe what you saw and, if appropriate, how that made you feel. You can then ask the individual if that is what they meant.
- *Use questions rather than statements.* Questions give the lawyer the responsibility of reaching their own conclusions and force them to think about the issues. For instance, you could ask 'How would you deal with it if one of your team members did what you did?'. Give them lots of opportunity to express what their intentions were and how these manifested themselves in the situation and whether these had the desired impact or not. The lawyer should be encouraged to think about how they could do something differently in future to achieve the required result.
- *Comparisons rather than condemnation.* Make evaluations against agreed criteria, past performance or competitive benchmarks. Identify high and low points of performance and specific behaviours which appear to contribute to or limit success. You can make suggestions here if they are appropriate, and might want to say what can be done in future to improve performance.
- *Good as well as bad.* Things that a law firm or lawyer do well, in addition to areas for improvement, are important – people need to feel encouraged. Get into the habit of commenting on what you like all the time – praise is a powerful energiser.
- *Agreed plan of action.* Formulate an agreed plan of action with the most important points from your discussion – which should be no more than three at a time. Ask how you can help to achieve the agreed plan. The feedback conversation is a two-way communication – ask how you can be of most value to the recipient. Be sure to act on points you have agreed.

Techniques for receiving feedback from external law firms

Do not be afraid. This is the point at which you learn something valuable about the impact you have in their world.

Review against your expectations. Does it line up with what you intended?

Listen. Listen quietly with no interruptions – just concentrate on what is being said.

Don't be defensive. Avoid the temptation to defend yourself. This is an opportunity for you to understand the impact of your communication – there will be time later to explain the intent.

Explore and understand what is being said. This doesn't necessarily mean you agree with it.

Encourage, don't punish. Remember, it is not easy for the law firms to do this, so encourage them, don't punish them. If you do, you will lose the respect and trust of that law firm and, once lost, it will be very difficult to retrieve.

Ask for more. Where appropriate, seek further feedback – if it's helpful, say so. Asking 'Are there any other areas in which this is causing a problem?' will encourage them to provide comprehensive information which will assist your own development by increasing your self-awareness.

Write it down. Make a summary statement of what you have heard to check for accuracy.

Respond honestly. You can express your honest opinion and feelings: 'I'm really surprised about these points so I will go away and give what you say some serious thought.'

Sense-check the response. Check it out with others whose opinions you value if the feedback comes as a surprise. Sometimes something may be an issue for one firm and not for another. Reflect on the past and observe yourself now.

Use the feedback to improve. Plan new behaviour patterns and seek support for your proposed actions, but only if you want to change and genuinely intend to do so. The choice is yours – but why would you waste the opportunity to learn from the feedback to enable you to manage and work with your external lawyers more effectively?

17 Communication skills

INTRODUCTION

You cannot help but communicate so why not do it on purpose/deliberately! Communication is not about your intention. It is about the impact of the:

- body language
- voice and tone
- language.

All three are utilised in communicating and influencing. The recipient of your communication will notice any incongruence you show between the three – whether they are your colleagues within the organisation, your external law firms or members of your team.

According to Professor Albert Mehrabian in his book *Silent Messages*, the balance of meaning through spoken communication is thus:

- 7 per cent of meaning is in the words that are spoken
- 38 per cent of meaning is paralinguistic (the way that the words are said)
- 55 per cent of meaning is in facial expression.

Each part can affect the meaning of the spoken word. Professor Mehrabian states that we should use this as a guide. If you are not clear then use the active listening skill of reflecting back your understanding and/or asking open questions to ensure clarity of meaning.

It is not enough to listen actively to others; you need to demonstrate that you are doing so. This is a very powerful and underused tool of communication.

Your own information filtering system will affect your ability to understand another's communication. It is easy to interpret words, tone or body language from your own beliefs, values and experiences. Your lack of attention can warp your understanding of the message being sent to you.

Communication techniques – giving information

Remember the constituents of communication. Communication is vital for all lawyers and Document 2 of Part III – Competencies for in-house lawyers

– details the vital ingredients to successful communication. It is worth reminding yourself of these before completing Exercise 6 in Part III – Communication habits – on your own communication habits:

- understand and use departmental and corporate communication systems
- express self orally and in writing
- understand and use information technology
- use and provide information to support decision making and problem solving
- be proactive in searching for, providing and sharing information
- present complex information logically, concisely and persuasively
- contribute to and/or lead meetings
- advise on and/or handle the media
- negotiate effectively
- encourage and provide feedback from and to all levels in the organisation
- establish information management and communication systems.

How do you use your organisation's and department's communication systems? Do you treat official briefings as a joke? On the other hand, open-door informality does not work if you are always too busy to stop to communicate with any one who ventures through. Conversations held when you are distracted by other matters hardly demonstrate your intention to be always available. Our recommendation is always to use the official lines of communication, but to supplement them with as much informality as your organisation will allow – this will encourage true sharing of information.

Remember, written can be best. The best medium for pure information and facts is written – people can read five times faster than you can talk. If you pass on this information verbally, you are only engaging your external lawyers with the content aimed primarily at the intellectual level. This means you are operating in a very narrow range and appealing most to the linear processing side of the brain. Obviously, if your written skills are not up to scratch then your written communications will not be as effective as they could be.

House styles. Have you recorded and shared the preferred house style to ensure continuity of written styles of communication for contracts, reports and briefings?

Identify your and their preferences. Find out which communication medium you and your law firms prefer, and share this with those with whom you want to communicate – paper, telephone, face to face. You will also want to look at the timing of communication – you may find that conversations in the early morning or late afternoon increase effectiveness, depending on the individual recipient concerned.

Communication styles. Remember there are various different methods of analysing communication styles – for example those used in the case study at the end of this chapter: 'helper', 'battler' and 'thinker'. Consider what communication style you use – particularly if your organisation has a method it prefers. The objective is to present information in the recipient's preferred style – mirroring that person's style aids effective communication.

Mirroring. Matching body movements, the pace of speech, phraseology used, voice sound and tone can aid communication significantly, and help create empathy between the parties.

Gender or cultural differences. A recent study conducted on the way women and men enter a room demonstrated the different use of body movement in communication. Women exhibited 27 distinct body movements compared with men displaying 12. When observers were asked to rate the estimated power or status of a person entering a room they gave a higher rating to those who made fewer movements. Be careful about the assumptions you can draw from communication differences between the genders and cultures. This is particularly true in making contact with each other; some cultures have strong views about such assumptions.

Focus. Keep your goals in mind and do not wander off the subject or repeat yourself. Be aware of possible short attention spans of your listeners.

Right- or left-brain activity. To move people to action, or persuade them to agree with your point of view, then you must engage their right brain. If you do not then you are missing much of your potential for impact to influence them. To be heard you need to engage their senses and their entire mind. To do this you must try to use examples matching words, drama, humour, visuals or movement.

Use your body language intentionally to provide congruence with your message. Do you know what passive, assertive or aggressive body language looks like? Check out your body language with a colleague or coach to establish which category it falls into and whether it corresponds with your message, or is at odds with it. For example, extremely fast small body movements – such as fiddling or touching your face – could impede a confident delivery of important information.

Body space. Ensure you understand and respect other persons' personal space – otherwise your actions could be perceived as aggressive at worst and insensitive at best. Check out the geography of space at meetings – ensuring that there is enough, but not too much as this will inhibit communication.

Eye contact. Use eye contact appropriately. In business meetings, generally, you will find that eye contact of around five seconds is appropriate. Normally people use five to ten seconds for one-to-one communication, and four to five seconds for individual contact in groups. If you find eye contact difficult, then this will seriously impede the effect of your communication. For example, if you are talking to someone while looking out of the window or around the room, you will probably find that they perceive that the communication and the person are not important to you.

Techniques for demonstrating listening

Demonstrate listening by giving full attention
- *using supportive eye contact* – not staring the other person down or looking at a computer screen (see the notes in the previous section on the effect and timing of eye contact)
- *paying careful, non-evaluative attention* to the lawyer's body language – their facial expression, gestures and body movements as

107

well as the words. You are looking for congruence or incongruence. When you see incongruence, it should alert you to ask more questions – there may well be more going on than is apparent from the speech

- *having an expectation of interest* in what the external law firm or lawyer wants to tell you – otherwise you may quickly become bored and lose interest
- *keeping your own internal dialogue to a minimum* – you will have expectations about what the other person is saying or what responses you are going to make to what you are hearing. These expectations may well stop you concentrating properly on what is being said. If you find it difficult to pay full attention, then repeat internally what is being said to you. This will also help you to recall what was said, and in what context.

Use matching supportive body movements and expressions to provide a warm, accepting atmosphere for free expression of thoughts, ideas, attitudes and values by:

Matching

- Conduct a workshop and/or conference around a methodology to identify the different styles of the internal and external lawyers so that communication can be matched to the style of the recipient e.g. analyst. There are plenty to choose from as well as the one chosen by Carillion set out in the case study to Part II.
- *giving confirming nods of your head*
- *giving confirmatory sounds* such as 'hmmm …', 'I see' or 'Go on …'
- *reinforcing* – choosing expressions to reinforce what has been said – 'Yes, you have hit the nail on the head!'
- *not being afraid of silence* – it is natural to pause, even in the middle of sentences, for three or four seconds, even though it may feel like twenty seconds in your mind
- *encouraging the other person to expand by asking open questions*
- *keeping your reaction appropriate and matched to the giver* – for instance, by using a measured pace appropriate to the type of communication being received
- *being aware of your tone* – an inappropriate tone will make it obvious that you are not really listening, but just going through the motions. Keep your voice well modulated to fit the content

- *not using judgemental words.* Any sentences containing words like 'should' or 'ought' should be watched – these ensure that the emotional content of your response is perceived as harsh and condemnatory despite any intention to the contrary.

Reflect back

Reflect what you have heard to demonstrate you have really listened to the lawyer by:

- *using the lawyer's name* when responding
- *using appropriate expressions* such as 'xxxx, I think this is what you are saying ... Am I correct?'
- *interrupting appropriately* – with a voluble talker you may have to interrupt to get the space to reflect. Use phrases like 'xxxx, can I just check I've understood the points so far?' This also gives you time to check your understanding before reacting
- *ensuring that you not do reflect back too many times* – this may mean that the recipient feels you are interrupting rather than confirming
- *considering benefits to the recipient* – how will what you say benefit the lawyer and encourage greater feedback and information?

Case study – Carillion's Fourth Annual Legal Network Conference 2006 – Service and Communication

At Carillion Legal, we like to think that we take a different approach to purchasing legal services. Our internal customers tell us that we are different. Our Network firms tell us that we are different. In preparing for our Fourth Annual Network Conference, we sought to use the opportunity for the conference to really make an impact upon the way in which Carillion's Legal Network operated, and to challenge ourselves to do something really different.

The conference had developed over the preceding years to include two consistent elements. The first was, effectively, information sharing. One of the things that sets our in-house lawyers apart from their counterparts in private practice is their intimate knowledge of the business and its functions. It is the insight and familiarity that they possess which enables them to provide truly business-focused solutions. Giving lawyers at our Carillion

Legal Network firms a similar understanding of our business – both in terms of its working and objectives – is crucial, since it assists them in formulating tailor-made advice and solutions. We have always considered it essential that our Carillion Legal Network firm lawyers start to understand our direction and strategy so that they can move forward to support our business effectively.

We knew from the formal feedback provided after each of the previous conferences that our external lawyers valued this feature of the conference highly. Hence we decided that 'Getting to know Carillion' would, in some form, once again be on the billing. As a company for whom constant change is the norm, we were content with this since there is always something new to tell our Carillion Legal Network firms.

The second of the two consistent elements that had featured in earlier conferences was a 'know-how' or 'technical skills' section. The format for this element had varied over the course of the three years, but a common denominator remained ever-present. This was a sharing of technical know-how relevant to Carillion's businesses – whether the emphasis was education, development of knowledge management or streamlining processes.

As a result of a stringent and thorough exercise at the time of the formation of the Network, we are able largely to take the quality and correctness of the technical legal advice that we receive from the Network firms for granted.

As important, though, is the ability of our in-house and external teams to communicate effectively. We understand that clear, effective communication is the cornerstone of providing most services and it is the very foundation of providing effective and efficient legal services. Yet all too often we also see that lawyers are so focused on the advice that is being given that there is a strong temptation to neglect the mode, method or style in which that advice is delivered.

Who would want their hand-finished, made-to-measure, one-off gown to be stuffed in a jiffy bag and delivered by second-class post? Far from promoting style over substance, by the time that the Carillion Legal Network was entering its fourth year, we had a confidence in our Carillion Legal Network firms that allowed us to take the decision to focus on what are often referred to as 'soft' skills.

For the fourth annual conference, we chose the theme of 'Service and Communication', believing that the two went hand in hand.

From early on in our preparations, we recognised that communication is a two-way street, and that the ability of Carillion's legal team and internal customers to communicate effectively was a necessary part of the package. We were very keen to ensure that an emphasis was placed on the concept of 'two-way' communication throughout the day. Hence, every exercise, session or workshop was structured to apply equally to Carillion personnel and to attendees from our Carillion Legal Network firms.

To help us deliver our position clearly, and to ensure that both internal and external teams received full benefit from the day, we decided to involve an external facilitator. As well as helping us to develop workshop sessions and exercises, the facilitator gave presentations to the conference delegates on styles of communication which were broadly aligned to three different personality types. This presentation followed an exercise where every attendee answered a bespoke questionnaire about their own style of communication and then, using their answers to those questions, placed themselves in one of three communication personality types – classified as 'thinker', 'battler' and 'helper'. Many of us shared two styles as a preferred element – and we explored how these contrary preferences changed the way we might be seen by our colleagues and others within our teams and the Network firms.

The work on 'communication personalities' was one of the highlights of the day. It was successful because not only did we have an expert speaking about a subject that applied equally to everyone in the room, but also because we had underestimated how much everyone would like hearing about themselves!

It also helped that the external facilitator was perceived as 'neutral' since this allowed him to raise questions and make observations that may have otherwise proved controversial.

The enthusiasm with which the main presentation was met spilled over into the first workshop session, where we saw the debate take off in an unusually short time. We felt that this was a good barometer of how the subject matter had been received by our delegates. In carefully selected teams, the delegates discussed their own personal communication styles, the limitations associated with these styles and identified whether there was a style which was common to their group.

Later in the day same delegates regrouped and discussed what could be done to address the limitations of their communication styles. In addition, they considered how they might enhance day-to-day communication in a sustained manner when supplying and purchasing legal services to and on behalf of Carillion.

Given that the theme of the day did not readily lend itself to a clear product or easily measurable change, we wanted to ensure that there was an 'output' from the day. Working with our external facilitator, we came up with the idea of a 'Communication Plan'. This was to span no more than two sides of A4, and was intended to act as a guide or charter by which Carillion and the Network firms would work over the coming years. Effectively, these Communication Plans were to consist of two-way promises, aims and ideals that had been agreed as a result of the workshops that had featured throughout the day.

We have encouraged our colleagues within Carillion and the Network firms to treat these documents as 'live'. We have asked that they pin them to a noticeboard or copy them to the person sitting next to them to ensure that they are not simply placed in a drawer to gather dust.

The theme of the conference was intended to be relevant to the stage of the development and improvement of the Network at that point in time. This made-to-measure approach ensured that we kept our audience fully engaged throughout the day and committed to the output – and focused on an understanding that the techniques for achieving the way in which our legal services are delivered are just as important as the services themselves.

Part III
The tools

The documents and exercises contained in this part are designed to help you think through some of the issues discussed in the previous parts of this book. These forms and precedents might prove helpful in deciding what to carry out in-house, and what and how to outsource to external providers. A number of these exercises have been already been tested in practice – at Carillion and at The Co-operative Bank p.l.c.

Exercises

1   P.E.S.T.L. analysis – political, economic, social, technological and legal factors
2   Legal activities to support the strategic plan
3   Legal services analysis
4   Personal assessment
5   S.W.O.T. analysis – strengths, weaknesses, opportunities and threats
6   Communication habits

Documents

1   Role of in-house lawyers – model of multi hats of in-house lawyers
2   Competencies for in-house lawyers
3   The DuPont Legal Model
4   Legal Strategy framework
5   Legal Exposure Plan framework
6   Service Level Agreement framework
7   Invitation to Tender framework
8   Carillion review scoring spreadsheet
9   Draft Relationship Protocol
10 Working Instructions Checklist

Exercise 1

P.E.S.T.L. analysis – political, economic, social, technological and legal factors

What is the P.E.S.T.L. analysis?

The P.E.S.T.L. analysis is very important in allowing an organisation to understand and align itself to its environment before beginning a process of identifying how it wishes to move forward. It achieves an analysis of the external factors affecting the business, and should be carried out continuously and used to support all aspects of your planning.
The organisation's external environment is made up from:

- the internal environment, e.g. staff or internal customers, office technology, wages and finance
- the micro-environment, e.g. external customers, agents and distributors, suppliers and competitors
- the macro-environment, e.g. political (and legal) forces, economic forces, sociocultural forces and technological forces
- it is now common in this complex regulatory world to add a fifth section, called legal, to capture the legal and regulatory forces both local and global.

We set out below some questions to start your own thinking or brainstorming on these topics. These are not meant to be a closed or comprehensive list – you should add other questions appropriate to your organisation and its environment.

1. Political factors

The political arena has a huge influence on the regulation of businesses, and the spending power of consumers and other businesses. Consider issues such as:

- How stable is the political environment?
- What is the government's position on marketing ethics?
- What is the government's policy on the economy?
- Does the government have a view on culture and religion?

2. Economic factors

Consider the state of the economy, and how it affects your organisation. Look at:

- interest rates
- the level of inflation
- employment level per capita
- long-term prospects for the economy
- gross domestic product (GDP) per capita
- the financial health of your sector, your organisation, the current market in which your organisation operates and any future ones it would like to access.

3. Sociocultural factors

The social and cultural influences on business vary from country to country. It is very important that such factors are considered. Factors to consider include the following:

- What is the dominant religion?
- What are attitudes to foreign products and services?
- Does language impact on the diffusion of products into markets?
- How much time do consumers have for leisure?
- What are the roles of men and women within society?
- How long is the population living? Are the older generations wealthy?
- Does the population have a strong/weak opinion on green issues?

4. Technological factors

Technology is vital for competitive advantage, and is a major driver of globalisation. Consider the following points:

- Does technology allow for products and services to be made more cheaply and to a better standard of quality for you and your organisation?
- Do the technologies available offer consumers and businesses more innovative products and services such as internet banking, new generation mobile telephones, and so on?
- How is distribution changed by new technologies, e.g. books via the internet, flight tickets, auctions, and so on?

- Does technology offer companies a new way to communicate with consumers?

5. Legal factors

You might want to consider the following:
- How stable is the legal and regulatory environment for your organisation?
- How stable is the legal and regulatory environment for the way you practise law for your organisation?
- What will the effect of the Legal Services Bill published in 2006 be on your organisation and/or department?
- How stable is the legal and regulatory environment for your external law firms and/or barristers and/or others, e.g. paralegals?
- Will government policy influence laws that regulate or tax your organisation?

P.E.S.T.L.

Political	Economic
Sociocultural	Technological
Legal	

Exercise 2
Legal activities to support the strategic plan

This exercise gives you the opportunity to relate three key areas to the day-to-day activities you and your team carry out.

Strategic

Q: Do you know the strategic goals for your organisation?
Q: What activities do you do that support these, and demonstrate your understanding of the business?

Corporate governance policy and control

Q: What central 'corporate governance' systems are in place?
Q: Are you part of that process and, if so, how?

Risk management

Q: What risk management policies and process are in place?
Q: What is the role of your in-house and external lawyers, and what should be the roles of your in-house and external lawyers?

Internal lawyers	External firm

Exercise 3

Legal service analysis

Ask each of your lawyers to complete this form, setting out the legal services they provide. You should then invite the whole team, or a selected group, to revisit each task to check the value to the business, and to identify whether a different way of delivering the task might be beneficial or more economic. It will also allow you to identify whether the task is required at all – changes over time may mean that it is not.

The last column is completed once you have analysis of the tasks. It may be that your organisation wants you to complete the specific tasks. In the example we show how the form might be completed in the case of a strategic international project while potentially saving money and maintaining headcount. It is assumed that a risk management process will have been utilised to assess the risks of moving or not doing the work.

Area of law	Specific tasks	Cost of these to the business	Different ways of providing and/or developing the service
1. Example: employment	1. Ensuring legislation compliance (1) 2. Training of HR (1). No training done for managers on employment matters. 3. Drafting contracts of employment, compromise agreements, etc. (1) 4. Employment policies updating	1. 5 PQE employment solicitor 2. External budget £150,000.	1. Compliance can be switched to internal audit department or a self-certification system – saving of at least 1 day per week. 2. Training on legislation and risk management can be provided by externals out of training and the new diversity project budget.

continued overleaf

Area of law	Specific tasks	Cost of these to the business	Different ways of providing and/or developing the service
	5. Handholding HR and managers in contentious employee disputes & and tribunal work (2) 6. A speaking slot at the employment away day and a standing invitation to their monthly management meetings. 7. On the project team for the HR intranet project which meets fortnightly. 8. Ad hoc advice for managers sent to both external (estimated £15K) and internal lawyers (1 day per week)		3. & 4. HR trained to do these with a value-driven supervisory overview by employment solicitor. 5. A small working party can be set up including HR legal & and external law firm on how to implement best practice and to reduce external spend, etc. 6. External speaking slot provided as part of the service by externals but internal lawyer continues attendance at meetings. 7. Changes project role to overseeing output and not attendance. 8. Ad hoc advice must now be given to HR who will filter the requests to internal lawyers who will decide if it needs to go out. An added bonus may be that by revisiting the specific tasks and evaluating how these can be done Legal can now become actively involved with the business and HR in developing and delivering a strategic international diversity programme to ensure consistency of

Area of law	Specific tasks	Cost of these to the business	Different ways of providing and/or developing the service
			values and compliance with local legislation, whilst not having to increase headcount for lawyers and possibly even reducing it.
2.			
3.			
4.			
5.			

Exercise 4

Personal assessment

This is a simple personal assessment for General Counsel or Department Heads to identify their technical, business and soft skills. You may want to collect feedback from designated peer groups, team members and your boss depending on the system used by your organisation.

	Strengths	Areas for improvement	Personal development (calendar year)
Technical			
Business			
Leadership			
Management			
Relationship management			
Soft skills			

This can be replicated for your in-house legal team *or* you can utilise any competency-based and/or soft skills-based assessment system used by your organisation.

Exercise 5

S.W.O.T. analysis – strengths, weaknesses, opportunities and threats

This is a really versatile exercise. You can use this exercise for your own career, team, for your organisation, your organisation's competitors and, last but not least, for your relationships with external law firms.

S.W.O.T. analysis is also known as T.O.W.S. analysis because you can start in the bottom two boxes and, once you understand the threats and opportunities, you can match the strengths and weaknesses against those.

Strengths and **weaknesses** are internal to you or your department or organisation. **Opportunities** and **threats** relate to external factors.

If you are having difficulty in identifying the strengths and weaknesses relevant to your situation, then try writing down a list of the characteristics you are analysing to enable you to consider whether these are a strength or not. Another good tip is, once you have your list, to compare it, where appropriate, with your impression of the strengths and weaknesses of your competitors. If any point is the same then it is not a strength but a necessity.

On examining opportunities and threats, you need to be aware of trends affecting your situation. As such, you may find that the P.E.S.T.L. analysis (see Exercise 1) is a good exercise to do first. You can then examine those factors to explore what opportunities and/or threats exist. Again, where appropriate, you should review what the competition is doing.

Strengths	**Weaknesses**
What do you do well?	What could you improve?
What do you/others see as your strengths?	What do you/others see as your weaknesses?
Opportunities	**Threats**
What realistically good opportunities are open to you?	What threats are you exposed to and can harm you?
How can you turn your strengths into opportunities?	How can you avoid these?

Exercise 6
Communication habits

In interpersonal communication, some habits will either enhance or detract from your effectiveness – for example, do you finish everyone's sentences?

Communication habit	Enhances your message	Detracts from or impedes your message

Document 1

Role of in-house lawyers – model of multi hats of in-house lawyers

Below is a figure which was originally produced by Bruce Macmillan, Senior Legal Adviser, Dell EMA and commented on by the C & I Group Corporate Governance Committee and Wragge and Co. LLP. It was first published in the seminal booklet *Reconciling the Irreconcilable? – Best practice guidelines for in-house lawyers in England and Wales in the new corporate governance environment* (C&I Group and Wragge and Co. LLP, March 2005).

Document 2
Competencies for in-house lawyers

Competencies describe the behaviours necessary for effective performance at work. They are a set of codified characteristics which research has shown to be associated with achieving successful outcomes in organisations.

The following are extracted from *Competencies for In-House Lawyers* compiled by the Law Society Commerce and Industry Group and the Centre for Dispute Resolution – CEDR. Ann Page was one of many in-house lawyers who contributed to this work. These are meant as a starting point for understanding and implementing successful behaviours.

Section One – Strategy/business acumen

- Understand internal structures and relationships
- Network, create and develop productive working relationships
- Identify and get the best from key stakeholders
- Develop commercial awareness of the internal and external environments
- Show awareness of future challenges to the organisation
- Generate ideas and solutions which add value to the business
- Promote the role of the legal department in adding value to the organisation
- Recognise and implement corporate values and ethos
- Take calculated risks to achieve business goals
- Contribute to the development, implementation, monitoring and review of corporate plans
- Evaluate areas where legal risk management would add most value

Section Two – Leadership

- Demonstrate commitment to the organisation's aims, values and strategy

- Use oral and written influencing skills
- Provide motivation
- Generate and encourage creative solutions to problems
- Focus on results
- Anticipate, facilitate and/or lead change
- Deal flexibly and confidently with the unexpected
- Adapt behaviour and style to the situation and competence of individuals
- Create and convey a clear vision of success

Section Three – Manage finances and resources

- Understand resources, budgets and constraints
- Use financial information
- Control expenditure against budgets
- Evaluate clients' needs and resources
- Support the efficient use of resources within the legal department and the organisation
- Make recommendations for departmental and organisational expenditure
- Determine the effective use of resources
- Set a budget

Section Four – Corporate/client relationships

- Promote legal department to widest possible internal client base
- Establish and agree corporate client requirements
- Manage corporate clients' needs and expectations
- Meet corporate client requirements
- Enable managers to recognise the need for in-house legal services
- Enable managers to identify and minimise legal risks
- Contribute to crisis management in the organisation
- Develop and implement quality assurance
- Manage complaints
- Manage relationships with 'regulators'

Section Five – Manage external lawyers and other professionals

- Develop productive working relationships
- Brief external lawyers/others
- Enable external service providers to understand internal corporate procedures
- Establish and agree your requirements with external lawyers/others
- Supervise and review progress and ensure agreed outcomes are achieved
- Manage costs
- Manage potential conflicts of interest
- Identify appropriate providers of external legal/other services, ensuring best value

Section Six – Manage individuals and/or teams

- Contribute to the recruitment and selection of personnel
- Plan, allocate and evaluate the work of teams and individuals
- Promote team working
- Contribute to the learning and development of teams and individuals
- Assess and provide feedback to teams and individuals on their performance
- Empower teams and individuals
- Delegate work to others
- Support individuals who have problems affecting their performance
- Deal positively and objectively with conflict
- Manage change

Section Seven – Communication

- Understand and use departmental and corporate communication systems
- Express self orally and in writing
- Understand and use information technology
- Use and provide information to support decision making and problem solving
- Be proactive in searching for, providing and sharing information
- Present complex information logically, concisely and persuasively

- Contribute to and/or lead meetings
- Advise on and/or handle the media
- Negotiate effectively
- Encourage and provide feedback from and to all levels in the organisation
- Establish information management and communication systems

Section Eight – Manage self

- Manage conflicting demands and priorities
- Demonstrate consistency and reason in decision making even when under pressure
- Act assertively
- Behave ethically and display integrity
- Actively seek and create challenging opportunities for self-development
- Participate in team working
- Learn to build own strengths and recognise and seek to improve weaknesses
- Keep abreast of key developments in law and legal practice
- Be open to change
- Be aware of and able to confront own prejudices
- Work within equalities policy and good-practice guidelines

Document 3
The DuPont Legal Model

General

We have not included the DuPont Legal Model in this book as most United Kingdom legal and company secretarial departments do not have the drivers which led to this model, nor do they have the same level of financial spend. However, it would be remiss of us not to bring this model to your attention. Full details are contained in their website www.dupontlegalmodel.com, which also sets out the basic premise of the Model:

'The Model is a comprehensive and integrated process that takes a business-focused and results-oriented approach to law, and helps law firms and corporate law departments improve the quality, cost and efficiency of legal service.'

The Model is being continuously improved and the site contains comprehensive information on it, and two helpful templates (engagement letter and request for a proposal). It also includes details of the latest book called *The Competitive Edge – The Growing Power of the DuPont Legal Model*. As we have not had access to the book we cannot comment on the contents. However, we can recommend the site to you.

We have extracted two tables which you may find of particular interest.

DuPont relationship managers

Below is a list of the functions' activities and the division between the Engagement Partner who has overall responsibility, and the day-to-day activities of the Account Manager.

Engagement Partner	Account Manager
Enlists firm's senior management support	Handles day-to-day program-related tasks and challenges
Has influence within the firm	Educates others
Allocates resources	Applies technology
Negotiates fee structures	Serves as primary network communications interface
Leverages the relationship	Participates in the annual review
Serves as foremost external advocate	Engages in Network activities
Seizes marketing opportunities for the firm	Initiates collaboration with other Primary Law Firms and service providers
Addresses internal compensation to reinforce best in class	Writes for external publications
Provides strategic thinking	Assists engagement partner with advocacy of the program within and elsewhere
Promotes technology investment	Supports supplier usage
Conducts annual reviews	
Focuses on women/minorities serving DuPont	

DuPont billing matrix

	Hourly rates	Blended rates	Flat fee/ fixed	Capped fees	Performance-based fees	Value billing
Risk of cost overruns	Entirely on client	Client	Law firm	Depends on the cap	Shared	Shared
Risk of adverse outcomes	Entirely on client	Client	Client	Client	Shared	Shared
Degree of trust required	Low	Medium	Medium	Medium	High	High
Alignment of objectives	Low	Low to medium	Medium	Medium	High	High

Document 4
Legal Strategy framework

6.   The future
7.   Responsibility, contact and review

Document 4 – Drafting notes

1.   See Chapter 1 for the role and importance of a legal strategy and the process to follow in preparing one for your organisation.
2.   This is one of your primary delegation documents as mentioned in Chapter 15.
3.   It is important to document what you do – and as important to document what you do not do or want to do.

Document 5
Legal Exposure Plan framework

1. Aims and objectives

We recognise that it is crucial that we provide effective customer service. The exposure of the legal team as a whole and its individual members is crucial to successfully marketing the legal team and our external law firms, and ensuring that the team has optimum profile within the various business divisions and within the Group as whole. This Exposure Plan sets out the methods by which the various sub-teams within Legal will seek to increase exposure and raise profiles over the next twelve months so as to have a positive effect on Legal's relationship with its internal customers.

Corporate

During the year we will:

- build sound working relationships at all levels and in all parts of the Group through our role of liaising and advising on regulatory and compliance matters
- arrange for the Legal Conference which will be attended by each member of the team and key representative from the external firms
- arrange training days for colleagues so they better understand our role and responsibilities
- maintain sound compliance systems so that bad publicity does not arise with external regulators
- raise colleagues' awareness of corporate governance and company law issues through presentations
- produce know-how briefings for the Legal intranet
- arrange for articles about Legal to appear in the next issue of our internal newspaper.

Knowledge management

During the year we will:
- keep our Legal intranet up to date and add: [define projected documents for the year]
- encourage team members and external lawyers to update their intranet profiles
- continue to provide training sessions and newsletters across the businesses.

Business Group A

- Meet new members of the business as part of the induction process
- Attend the business group's weekly team meetings
- Work on the development of the business's corporate governance procedures
- Initiate a process of documenting and reviewing commercial positions within the business
- Deliver training to commercial colleagues – internally or with external firms
- Offer support of extra lawyers seconded from the external firms
- Carry out 'Lessons Learned' exercises, also involving colleagues from the relevant business unit at the end of major projects or deals
- Second staff to other parts of the business or legal department
- Become more visible to external partners, clients and other advisers of the business unit

Business Group B

- Attend Management Team meetings
- Attend Business Review meetings
- Have a regular presence at the business unit's main site office
- Become more visible to external partners, clients and other advisers of the business unit
- Undertake site visits, presentations and safety tours
- Utilise one-to-one coaching (or small groups)
- Complete the development of the standard suite of supply chain documentation

[Repeat for each Business Group]

External law firms

Work with external law firms to:
- access know-how
- ensure all agreed value-adding activities and 'extras' are being provided
- carry out required reviews and feed back to the businesses.

Review

This Legal Exposure Plan will be reviewed annually

[Date]

[Originator]

Document 5 – Drafting notes

1. Identify how you want to make your internal and external lawyers visible within the business.
2. Use this document as a framework to plan for that.

Document 6
Service Level Agreement framework

Service Level Agreement – service level provided by Group Legal

Introduction

This agreement sets out the services provided by Group Legal, and the performance criteria which it will observe in providing those services.

Contacts

The primary contacts within Group Legal are:

[ ]	–	General Counsel
[ ]	–	Solicitor, Business Group A
[ ]	–	Solicitor, Business Group B
[ ]	–	Solicitor, Business Group C

In an emergency, out of office hours, contact should be made by the department's emergency number, which is [   ].

Service scope

Group Legal will provide a professional and timely legal service to the group and its UK businesses, either through self-delivery or through the instruction and management of external lawyers.

Objectives

Group Legal will have the following objectives in delivering the service:

- allocate appropriate resource within agreed time
- work in accordance with the agreed Legal Strategy
- fully inform colleagues during the work
- provide facilities for continuous development and feedback.

Operating principles

Group Legal will apply the following principles in delivering the service:
- work will be delivered in accordance with the agreed Legal Strategy
- reports will be delivered monthly in an agreed format
- the Lexcel registration will be used as the basis of our performance
- a named contact will be nominated for each piece of work
- a named supervisor will be nominated for each piece of work.

Activities

- Corporate law
- Litigation
- Property law
- Employment law
- Health, safety and environment
- Intellectual property
- [Add other specialist areas provided here]

Operating hours

Group Legal services are provided during normal working hours. Where necessary, work will be carried out outside of normal working hours subject to available resources. External resources can be provided if appropriate, subject to agreement of budget.

Reporting and monitoring

Group Legal will provide a monthly report to each business group in respect of the work carried out for that group. We will issue our report no later than one week after the end of the relevant month.

Measures of service level

Group Legal will seek to achieve the following service levels:
1. Return of calls: [ ] hours
2. Acknowledgement of emails or correspondence: [ ] hours
3. Substantive response: [ ] days

4. Report work progress: monthly or otherwise as agreed
5. Instruct externally if needed: [   ] days

Complaints

If customer satisfaction is not achieved, complaints should be made to the normal contact person. If this does not deal with the position satisfactorily, the matter may be drawn to the attention of the Business Group Solicitor and then, if still required, the General Counsel.

Review of this Service Level Agreement

This Service Level Agreement will be reviewed annually.

SIGNED: BUSINESS GROUP MANAGING DIRECTOR A

BUSINESS GROUP MANAGING DIRECTOR B

BUSINESS GROUP MANAGING DIRECTOR C

GENERAL COUNSEL

DATED:

Document 6 – Drafting notes

1. The framework must be adapted to the specific needs of your organisation.
2. Ensure you can deliver what you and your external lawyers promise in the Service Level Agreement – do not promise what cannot be achieved, or on the other hand hide what you can actually do.
3. Ensure that your external law firm contract, letter of instruction or protocol is back-to-back with any service level agreement you enter into.

Document 7

Invitation to Tender framework

Section	Subject
1.	**Introduction** • Reasoning behind tender • Historical position • Why recipients have been chosen • What you are trying to achieve • How you expect to run the process • What to do about queries
2.	**Company information** • What the company does • Parent and subsidiary information • Present legal work — amount, type, approximate costs • Who will instruct and how • What type of work is likely
3.	**Legal department** • Size, scale and role of legal department • How you will deal with external lawyers • What reporting you expect • Legal department role v. business groups • Future working relationships • Know--how and documentation
4.	**Approach to supply chain management** • How the organisation approaches supply chain management • What this means for lawyers • Reporting, measurement, management • Protocols, key performance indicators, written arrangements • How the tender will be run • How often the tender arrangements will be reviewed in the future

continued overleaf

Section	Subject
5.	**Future arrangements** • What are you looking for? • How many firms? • What will they do? • What is the period of the proposals? • What are your priorities? • What else do tendering firms need to know?
6.	**Legal network arrangements** • How will your new firm arrangements apply? • Reporting • Performance evaluation • Briefing and induction • Extras required • Operational issues and expectations
7.	**Fees and charging arrangements** • What proposals do you require? • If you want hourly rates, what for? • How often are they reviewed? • What about other arrangements – fixed, capped, blended rates? • Alternative billing arrangements • When will bills be rendered and paid? Drafts first?
8.	**Communication and reporting** • Set out what you want so expectations are clear • How are instructions given? • What are the communication chains? • What sort of reporting is required? • What happens when things go wrong? • Ending the relationship
9.	**Selection and evaluation criteria** • Define the selection and evaluation criteria in detail • Set out how the selection and evaluation criteria will be operated • Offer feedback

Section	Subject
10.	**Instructions** • Set out in detail what you want the tendering firm to do • Do you want written presentations, personal meetings or a combination? • Who do you want to meet? • Do you want a full marketing performance or limited information? • How are queries to be dealt with? • Who is the contact point?
Appendix 1	**Information required** • List all information required in tabular form so you can compare responses
Appendix 2	**Schedule of hourly rates** • If you are doing any work on hourly rates, seek a schedule against each level of qualification – e.g. newly qualified, 0–2 years, 3–5, 5–7, junior and senior partner levels

Document 7 – Drafting notes

1. If your organisation has a template Invitation to Tender document why not use that as a basis?
2. Work with your procurement, supply chain or purchasing department, if you have one. They will be used to procuring in other services and may well have been involved in outsourcing other professional services such as finance or human resources.
3. Consider what your target firms need to know and record it.
4. Be clear on what you want from the target firms – and specify it clearly.

Document 8

Carillion review scoring spreadsheet

	Firm 1	Firm 2	Firm 3	Firm 4	Firm 5	Firm 6	Firm 7	Firm 8	Firm 9	Firm 10
Price and value										
Market reputation										
Brand										
Experience										
Accessibility										
Service and delivery										
Team members										
Values										
Cultural fit										
Value-added services										
TOTAL										

Maximum score: 10 points per category; 100 total per firm.

Document 8 – Drafting notes

1. This spreadsheet is a format used by Carillion to score firms.
2. You should review the criteria against your own requirements and substitute those which suit you. You may also want to weight some categories – so some which are important to you score more than 10, others which are less vital, less than 10.
3. The sheet should be given to all those involved in considering presentations or tender documents to ensure consistency of review, marking and scoring.

Document 9
Draft Relationship Protocol

[Contact partner]
Dear [   ]

Protocol for our working relationship

1. **Introduction**
1.1   I write to set out a clear basic protocol for our business relationship for the provision of legal services to us. The arrangements set out in this letter will apply with effect from [date].
1.2   The quality of our legal services is of critical importance to us, and we believe that a clear understanding of the needs and expectations of both client and legal adviser is important if we are to achieve the most benefit from your advice.

2. **Areas of work**
2.1   I am pleased to confirm that you have been retained to provide advice in the following specialism(s):
      [list specialisms]
2.2   In addition, we may from time to time ask you to provide advice in other specialisms which we may discuss with you.
2.3   We will keep your performance under review and will meet at least every six months formally to review your work and the way in which this protocol has operated. We will ask that, one week before each of these meetings, you produce a short review document, setting out:
   • a summary of your present work for us
   • your fees in the year to date
   • your budgeted fees and work in progress
   • a self-assessment of your performance (including your performance against any action plans)
   • the ways in which you consider you are adding value
   • what we could both do to improve our working relationship

- any relevant personnel changes within your firm – actual and prospective
- any other issues which you would like to discuss at the meeting.

3.   Instructions

3.1   **Primary contact(s).** In all dealings, you should regard the person identified at Appendix 1 as your primary contact for the specific practice area(s) indicated.

In any other case, or if any matters require clarification, please address your query in the first instance to the senior lawyer in the relevant Business Group, or to me.

3.2   **Accepting instructions.** You may accept instructions from the people set out in Appendix 2. Those instructions may take the form of a letter, an email or a telephone call.

3.3   **Day-to-day contacts.** When you are initially instructed, your instructing member of staff (the 'Instructing Person') will tell you which staff you may contact. You may also contact me, or any of the lawyers in the relevant business group, at any time. If you need to contact anyone else, please ask the Instructing Person before doing so.

3.4   **Emergency contact.** In case of emergency out of business hours you may contact the Emergency Contact identified at Appendix 1. We have agreed that in turn we may contact the Emergency Firm Contact between us or utilise the emergency contact arrangements agreed between us from time to time.

4.   Specific protocol

4.1   The detailed provisions set out in Appendix 3 (if any) will apply to the provision of your work in your specialist area.

5.   Know-how

5.1   We may ask that from time to time you contribute to our knowledge management arrangements, generally by addition to our legal matter management system or legal intranet site by, for example:

   (a) updating guidance and information notes
   (b) providing know-how on specific work you have carried out for us, and
   (c) other material agreed between us.

6.   Strategy

6.1   We look at legal matters in a way that allows us to achieve the most satisfactory business solution, rather than in a purely academic way.

We also budget for the financial consequences of a transaction or other legal matter, and plan for the resources and key decisions involved.

6.2   To allow us to do this, before you commence any substantive work on a matter please produce a strategic plan and forward it to the Instructing Person. In the case of contentious matters, you should refer to our requirements set out at Appendix 4 and for non-contentious matters, our requirements set out at Appendix 5.

6.3   We would expect you to keep the strategic plan under review and to update it where necessary, at key points, as the matter progresses. It may well be necessary to revise it several times as the transaction proceeds. Our objective is to ensure that we understand enough of the legal background and cost issues to be in a position fully to support you in helping us achieve our business objectives.

6.4   We expect to be made aware of all significant steps in any transaction.

7.   **Costs**

7.1   **Cost basis.** The hourly rates that we have agreed with you are attached. We have agreed that any amendment to these rates will be by agreement with me from time to time. We expect that you will draw our attention to material issues which are not included in your budget.

7.2   **Agreement.** We expect the fee basis for all matters to be agreed before you begin work. We expect that the fee basis will be one of the following:

(a) an hourly rate on the cost basis set out in Appendix 6, subject to any cap we agree as appropriate which must not be exceeded without prior agreement in writing; or

(b) a fixed or capped fee, or

(c) any other fee charging arrangement that we agree with you, which may include conditional fees, contingency fees or risk-sharing arrangements

7.3   **Value of work.** As you know, as an overriding requirement, we look to you to provide us with legal services which are of commercial benefit to our business operations. Accordingly, the fee must never exceed the value to us of the work and you must ensure at all times that you are conscious of the way we wish to proceed.

7.4   **Expenses.** We have agreed:

(a) you will not, without our agreement, apply any mark-ups to any hourly rate agreed or to any disbursements incurred in any of our matters

(b) your hourly rate includes provision for all office and other overheads, including postage, telephones, faxes, couriers and photocopying, unless we agree otherwise for particular expenses in specific cases; and we will pay reasonable transport and accommodation costs (disbursements) incurred should you need to travel on our behalf. You will abide by our normal travel and expenses policy for our organisation's staff, as amended from time to time.

8. Billing

8.1 If we instruct you in any matter and total costs on the matter are anticipated to exceed £[   ], please provide us with draft bills for approval on a monthly basis unless we agree otherwise. You should not render a bill which has not been approved by us.

8.2 You should provide a commentary with your draft bill which sets out a breakdown and short description of the work done, the fee earner concerned, the number of hours spent, and the name of the relevant manager and/or lawyer who is instructing you. Unless otherwise agreed, we expect that all bills will be supported by a full analysis of tasks completed and time spent by whom. We may ask to have reasonable access to your time-recording records.

9. Staffing

9.1 We agree that the Relationship Partner identified at Appendix 1 has overall responsibility for those of our affairs on which we instruct you to act on our behalf. His or her role should be to keep a 'watching brief' on our matters, ensure that you handle them expeditiously, and that you identify and address the key issues. Each matter should have a lead lawyer, agreed with us, who need not be the Relationship Partner.

9.2 Subject to the following paragraph, we have agreed that people you will use on our matters will be drawn from the Firm Contacts set out at Appendix 1, or such other members of your team as you introduce to us from time to time by agreement with the Primary Contact on [insert specialism] matters.

9.3 We expect that you will use staff of an appropriate level on our matters. We expect to agree with you who you will use on a particular matter and that new staff should not be used without our prior agreement. Since continuity is important to us, you must tell us if you propose to change staff, and must not do so without our consent. If you need to change or add new staff, naturally we will not expect to pay for the time they will inevitably spend in familiarisation with the matter.

9.4 We try to achieve high standards in our business and look for similar standards in our advisers. As a normal rule, please try to ensure that correspondence, telephone calls and emails are dealt with/responded to within a reasonable time and, in any event, within the same working day.

10. Documentation

10.1 Please obtain our approval to all major documentation, instructions and briefs to Counsel, and to draft pleadings in significant litigation matters. Please also do not instruct Counsel without our approval. In giving such approval we will want to know his or her identity, and the reason for such instruction. We would like you to provide us with copies of all advices and opinions of Counsel.

10.2 Please copy the Instructing Person with all significant correspondence in any matter unless we ask you not to do so.

11. Reporting and review

11.1 Please provide us with a monthly report on all issues that you handle for us. We will ask that [insert specialism] matters are also reported to the primary [insert specialism] contact. Please report in the format we agree from time to time.

12. Training and education

12.1 It is important that the Company's legal health is regarded as critical and this is best achieved by ensuring that managers are provided with good documentation, satisfactory systems and an understanding of the legal issues affecting their business. We have agreed that you will provide for us training of such kinds as we agree from time to time.

12.2 We hope that you will increase your familiarity with our business as we work together. If you feel there are ways in which you could help us to achieve our objectives which are not the subject of specific instructions, you should always feel at liberty to discuss them with us.

13. Conflicts of interest

13.1 We understand that you must abide by the Law Society's guidelines on conflicts of interest in force from time to time. We also expect that you will not act against us in any matter without our prior agreement, which will not usually be forthcoming in the case of any litigation or dispute.

13.2   We ask that we are your client of choice, and that you should not accept instructions on any matter in which you reasonably believe we are likely to be interested without first ascertaining whether you are to be instructed by the Company.

14.   Media and other contact

14.1   We have agreed that any contact with you from the media or a member of the public in relation to our affairs should be immediately reported to us. You will not make any communication with the media or a member of the public without our express consent.

15.   Working practices

15.1   We have agreed that the working practices set out in this section will apply.

15.2   We ask that you circulate to all members of your team the Working Instructions Checklist attached at Appendix 7 to ensure that everyone is clear on our way of working.

15.3   We ask that your preferred method of communication with us is by email, and that we receive copies of documents by email wherever possible.

15.4   We value and welcome your feedback on our work, and we would ask that you provide written feedback to us on any areas where you feel we can improve.

16.   Confidentiality

16.1   The terms of our agreement shall be kept confidential and not disclosed by either of us to any third party without prior agreement.

17.   Entire agreement

17.1   This protocol sets out the entire agreement between the organisation and your law firm. Any amendment or alteration to the terms of this protocol must be in writing and signed by the General Counsel and the Relationship Partner. Specifically, no general terms and conditions of business of the law firm, or similar arrangements, will apply unless specifically agreed in writing by the General Counsel and the Relationship Partner.

You should refer any queries on this letter to me. Any queries on matters current at any time, or on any letter of instruction, should be referred to me.

If at any time you are unclear about any issue, or wish to discuss any aspect of the transaction, please telephone and we will do all we can to respond promptly and clearly to answer your concerns.

Yours sincerely

General Counsel

Appendix 1   Contact details
Appendix 2   **People from whom you may accept instructions**
Appendix 3   **Specialist area protocol provisions**
Appendix 4   **Strategic plan – contentious matters**
                    Initial preliminary assessment
                    Decisions and assumptions
                    Costs and resources
                    Consequences
Appendix 5   **Strategic plan – non-contentious matters**
                    Initial preliminary assessment
                    Decisions and assumptions
                    Costs and resources
                    Consequences
Appendix 6   **Agreed hourly rates**
Appendix 7   **Working Instructions Checklist**

Document 10
Working Instructions Checklist

The protocol describes how our legal services must be delivered. This checklist is intended to be a summary of the key principles which underlie the protocol.

1. Reporting

Your overriding reporting obligation is to the named Primary Contact in Appendix [   ], although you may accept instructions from any person named in Appendix [   ] ('the Instructing Person').

Protocol clause:

Reference:

You must ensure that the relevant Instructing Person is kept up to date with progress in the matter and is involved in all strategic and other important decisions. All significant documentation must be copied to the Instructing Person.

The Instructing Person will identify the commercial staff to be involved in the matter and their respective role(s). In case of doubt, please refer to the Primary Contact.

A monthly report in agreed form must be prepared and delivered to the Primary Contact and the Instructing Person during the first week of each month for all live matters.

The relevant Instructing Person must approve in advance all fee-earning staff working on matters, including any changes of staff.

2. Strategic direction

A clear strategic plan must be developed for each matter at the outset. The plan must be kept under review and updated as necessary during the currency of the matter.

*Protocol
clause:*

Reference:

Each strategic plan will contain the information set out in Appendix [ ] (Contentious matters) or Appendix [ ] (Non-contentious matters). Where, exceptionally for any reason, it would not be appropriate to prepare the plan at the outset (either in whole or in part), this must be agreed with the Instructing Person and the remainder of the plan completed as soon as possible.

The strategic plan must be kept under regular review and any necessary changes in strategic direction discussed and agreed with the Instructing Person.

3. No surprises

Except in emergencies, no legal work may be carried out unless an appropriate fee basis and budget has been discussed and agreed with the relevant Instructing Person.

*Protocol
clause:*

Reference:

The agreed charging rates apply to all work save where a fixed fee or other special arrangement has been agreed. Any budgeted amount must not be exceeded without the written approval of the Instructing Person.

Agreed rules apply to the charging of trainee time and disbursements, in particular travelling expenses (including time charges while travelling and waiting) and photocopying, phone, etc.

The strategic plan must contain an estimate of costs. The estimate must be kept under regular review and any changes agreed with the

154

person instructing you. Performance against the cost estimate must be reviewed in the monthly report. Reasons for variance to budget must also be explained.

The work carried out must be of commercial benefit to us – both in general, and in relation to specific items of work. If you are in any doubt you must discuss it with the relevant Primary Contact.

4. Billing

Protocol clause:

Reference:

A draft bill must be submitted for prior approval unless otherwise agreed. Where costs on a matter exceed a pre-agreed level, you must advice the Primary Contact at once.

Draft bills are to be submitted for approval on a monthly basis.

All bills must be presented in the agreed format, including a breakdown of work done, time spent, the fee earners concerned and disbursements.

5. Working practices

Protocol clause:

Reference:

At the conclusion of any non-contentious matters a précis must be prepared free of charge for staff operating the contract. For contentious matters, and for corporate transactions, a 'lessons learnt' report will be required.

A post-transaction review will be carried out using our post-transaction questionnaire.

[Date]

[Originator]

Document 11

Carillion key performance indicator set

Key Performance Indicators – measures for Carillion Legal

These indicators measure aspects of the performance of Carillion Legal:

A.   Financial

A1.1   **Costs of department v. external legal spend**
Cost of the department during the period: £[   ]
External legal spend with the Carillion Legal Network, excluding disbursements and VAT, and excluding spend on non-Network firms: £[   ]
Ratio of internal to external spend: [   ] or [   ]%

A2.1   **Value of client work as a multiple of department cost**
Value of client work carried out by the department, on the basis of an audit carried out by members of Legal during the period and extrapolated: £[   ]m
Cost of the department during the period: £[   ]
Value of client work as a multiple of department cost: [   ] times

A2.2   **Number of key matters requiring lawyer involvement per lawyer of value exceeding £10m**
The number of key matters requiring lawyer involvement per lawyer of value exceeding £10m in the period: [   ]

B.   Customer service

B1.1   **Client survey**
We carry out an on-going client survey using a feedback questionnaire available to all users of legal services through our intranet site. The survey asks more than 25 questions in the following categories:

- service quality
- programme and delivery
- co-operation and teamwork
- communication
- commerciality
- external lawyer management.

Rating score in period: [   ]%

Highest Network firm score in period: [   ]%

Average Network firm score in period: [   ]%

B1.2   Relationship audits

Relationship audits are carried out every six months by planned meetings between the Director of Legal Services, the Legal Director for each business group and the business group Managing Director. Number of audits carried out in the period for each business group: [   ]

B2.1   Number of training courses or workshops delivered by or through Carillion Legal in the period

Number of training courses or workshops by Carillion Legal in the period: [   ]

Number of training courses or workshops carried out by Network firms in the period: [   ]

B2.2   Number of people trained in the period

The number of people trained in the period: [   ]

C.   Business processes

C1.1   Number of post-completion reviews and contract briefing summaries provided

We seek to carry out post-completion reviews of major matters and transactions, and provide contract briefing summaries on matters of importance where possible:

Number of post-completion reviews carried out: [   ]

Number of contract briefing summaries provided: [   ]

C2.1   Number of precedents reviewed and added to our matter management system

We seek to enhance the Group's legal and commercial know-how by providing precedent documents for us and, where appropriate, our commercial colleagues to utilise.

Number of precedents reviewed and added to our matter management system: [   ]

C2.2 **Number of new matters entered onto our matter management system**
While the number of matters entered onto our system does not capture the value of our work, it will become a useful indicator of the volume of work carried out by Carillion Legal.
Number of new matters entered onto our matter management system: [   ]

C3.1 **Delivery of monthly report**
This indicator measures the percentage of monthly reports delivered on time from members of the team to the Director of Legal Services. It is important as it allows the ongoing reporting of key issues to the Board and Executive Directors.
Percentage of monthly reports delivered on time: [   ]%

D.   Lawyer satisfaction

D1.   **Employee turnover – percentage of replacement lawyers required**
This indicator measures turnover amongst the qualified staff in the team.
Number of lawyers leaving the team: [   ]
Percentage of lawyers leaving the team: [   ]%

Key performance indicators – measures for the Carillion Legal Network

A.   Financial

A1.1   **Actual cost of work v. estimate**
This is measured by a random sample of cases. In the sample taken, actual cost of the work against the estimate: [   ] %

A1.2   **Accuracy of case plan, efficiency, transparency of cost information and cost-consciousness**
These issues are subjective, and are monitored in two ways. First, by way of regular meetings with each member firm of the Network and, second, by way of intranet feedback.

**B.	Partnering**

B1.	Added value

We measure the number of added-value extras given or offered by each of the Network firms in the period. These range from seminars, newsletters, workshops and help lines to secondments and placings. They are measured by the Director of Legal Services and help to identify trends amongst the Network firms to genuine partnership with Carillion. Although the value of such issues will vary in monetary terms, the measure is useful to highlight individual performance of each firm.

In the period, average number of such arrangements, per firm: [   ]

B2.	Understanding our needs

We seek to identify how well each law firm understands our needs – our cultures, values, approach, business objectives and internal relationships, with a view to establishing long-term relationships and achieving better, smarter and faster results.

We measure these issues by discussions with our colleagues within Carillion, and by our intranet feedback form. The detailed results are set out in respect of C1, below.

**C.	Customer service**

C1.	Service quality

We carry out an ongoing client survey using a feedback questionnaire available to all users of legal services through our intranet site (see Document 12). The survey asks more than 25 questions in the following categories:

- service quality
- programme and delivery
- co-operation and teamwork
- communication
- commerciality.

In reviewing the scores, it is necessary to bear in mind that different individuals within the business will have been responsible for entering scores, that the number of individuals using some firms or the number of matters involved will be small and not create a meaningful sample, and that individual assessments of standards will vary. This indicator will be used most effectively to identify trends as monitoring progresses, so that if firms slip down the rating, it is possible to identify and challenge the reasons.

Network firm scores in the period: [   ]

D.   Business processes

D1.1   **Report quality – frequency of reports received on time**
Percentage of regular reports received on time from the Legal Network firms in the period: [   ]%

D1.2   **Appropriateness of reports**
The Director of Legal Services monitors and reviews the appropriateness of reports on a regular basis.

D2.   **Billing quality – accuracy and timeliness**
A random survey is carried out on a sample of bills to check their accuracy against a number of criteria, including compliance with protocol, compliance with the approved draft and (where charged on an hourly basis) compliance with time records and approved Carillion hourly rates.

Number of bills checked in this level of detail in the period: [   ]

Key performance indicators – numerical measures: internal

Indicator		Measure
A1.1	Cost of department	£
A1.2	External spend	£
A1.3	Ratio department/external	%
A2.1	Ratio client work as multiple of department cost	
A2.2	Number of key matters per lawyer over £10m	
B1.1	Client survey score	%
B2.1	Number of training courses delivered by Carillion Legal	
B2.1	Number of training courses delivered by Network firms	
B2.2	Number of people trained in the period	
C1.1	Number of post-completion reviews carried out	
C1.2	Number of contract briefing summaries provided	
C2.1	Number of precedents reviewed and added to our matter management system	

Indicator		Measure
C2.2	Number of new matters on matter management system	
C3.1	Delivery of monthly report	%
D.	Lawyer satisfaction – turnover	%

Key performance indicators – numerical measures: external

Indicator		Measure
A1.1	Actual cost of work v. estimate	%
B.	Number of added value extras per firm – average	
C.	Service quality – average Details and range: [ ]	%
D1.1	Frequency of reports on time	%
D2.	Number of bills checked in detailed audit	

Document 12

Carillion online survey feedback questionnaire

1. Service quality – score responses for each firm (and Carillion Legal) on a scale of 1–5	
(i)	Provided a skilful and professional service
(ii)	Provided a reliable and responsive service
(iii)	Produced accurate and high-quality documents
(iv)	Provided effective supervision with clear points of contact
2. Programme/delivery	
(i)	Project delivery/programme dates met
(ii)	Documents and advice produced to programme
(iii)	Requests for instructions made in a timely manner
(iv)	Correct resource levels given to the project
3. Co-operation/teamwork	
(i)	Built relationships of trust
(ii)	Used Carillion personnel effectively
(iii)	Explained steps to be taken in project/matter
(iv)	Related well to you as a client
4. Communication	
(i)	Accessible for discussions/meetings
(ii)	Effective communication at client level
(iii)	Effective communication with external parties
(iv)	Explained issues without use of jargon
5. Commercial	
(i)	Demonstrated an understanding of the business requirements
(ii)	Provided practical legal solutions to meet the business requirements
(iii)	Added value to the business
(iv)	Gave you the information needed to comply with your legal requirements

6. Financial management	
(i)	Effective planning of legal costs
(ii)	Provided sufficient transparency of information on costs
(iii)	Work undertaken at the right level
(iv)	Demonstrated commitment to manage costs
7. Network firm relationship	
(i)	Demonstrated commitment to Legal Protocol
(ii)	Demonstrated commitment to Carillion values
(iii)	Showed an interest beyond the specifics of the task
(iv)	Offered additional services at no extra cost
8. General	
(i)	Overall, you would rate the service very highly

Document 13
Network firm half-yearly feedback form

Feedback on Network firms – [name of firm]		Date	
Scores are based on a range of responses:			
100% – Strongly Agree > Agree > Disagree > Strongly Disagree – 0%			

1. Service quality		Your score	All Firms
(i)	Provided a skilful and professional service		
(ii)	Provided a reliable and responsive service		
(iii)	Produced accurate and high-quality documents		
(iv)	Provided effective supervision with clear points of contact		
2. Programme/delivery			
(i)	Project delivery/programme dates met		
(ii)	Documents and advice produced to programme		
(iii)	Requests for instructions made in a timely manner		
(iv)	Correct resource levels given to the project		
3. Co-operation/teamwork			
(i)	Built relationships of trust		
(ii)	Used Carillion personnel effectively		
(iii)	Explained steps to be taken in project/matter		
(iv)	Related well to you as a client		
4. Communication			
(i)	Accessible for discussions/meetings		
(ii)	Effective communication at client level		
(iii)	Effective communication with external parties		
(iv)	Explained issues without use of jargon		

5. Commercial		Your score	All Firms
(i)	Demonstrated an understanding of the business requirements		
(ii)	Provided practical legal solutions to meet the business requirements		
(iii)	Added value to the business		
(iv)	Gave you the information needed to comply with your legal requirements		
6. Financial management			
(i)	Effective planning of legal costs		
(ii)	Provided sufficient transparency of information on costs		
(iii)	Work undertaken at the right level		
(iv)	Demonstrated commitment to manage costs		
7. Network firm relationship			
(i)	Demonstrated commitment to Legal Protocol		
(ii)	Demonstrated commitment to Carillion values		
(iii)	Showed an interest beyond the specifics of the task		
(iv)	Offered additional services at no extra cost		
8. General			
(i)	Overall, you would rate the service very highly		

Document 14

Annual fees spreadsheet

	Q1			Q2			Q3			Q4			TOTAL
	Fees	Disbs	WIP	Fees	Disbs	WIP	Fees	Disbs	WIP	Fees	Disbs	WIP	
Firm 1													
Firm 2													
Firm 3													
Firm 4													
Firm 5													
Firm 6													
Firm 7													
Firm 8													
Firm 9													
Firm 10													
Firm 11													
Firm 12													
TOTAL													

Document 14 – drafting notes

1. Decide what you are measuring and use a consistent basis – for example, record your numbers:
   - with or without VAT
   - all or your share of joint venture costs
   - whether or not you are recording costs which can be recovered from a third party.
2. It may be helpful to get your law firm(s) to provide data to reconcile against your own.
3. It is suggested you record work in progress so you know what work the firm may wish to charge you for in the next quarter.
4. The information can be used to monitor trends in costs between firms.

Document 15

Trends spreadsheet

Work type	Year 1 Q1	Q2	Q3	Q4	Year 2 Q1	Q2	Q3	Q4	Year 3 Q1	Q2	Q3	Q4	Totals
Property													
Litigation													
Banking													
Construction													
Corporate													
Employment													
IP/IT													
Competition													
Pensions													
Other													
TOTALS													

Document 15 – drafting notes

1. Decide what you are measuring and use a consistent basis – with or without VAT, all or your share of joint venture costs, whether or not you are recording costs which can be recovered from a third party.
2. It may be helpful to get your law firm(s) to provide data to reconcile against your own.
3. The information can be used to monitor trends in types of work to identify changes in needs for resource or other arrangements.

Document 16
Post-transaction questionnaire

This questionnaire should be completed after each transaction or matter with a value of more than £[   ] or a fee cost of more than £[   ] has been completed.

The results of the questionnaire should then be aggregated and used to facilitate a post-transaction review between the organisation and the law firm.

A. Financial
1. What was the cost of the work?
2. How did this compare with the estimate?
3. How accurate was the case plan and cost information?
4. How cost-conscious was the law firm?

B. Understanding
1. How well did the law firm understand our business objectives?
2. How well did the relationship between us work?
3. Did the law firm work to our values and style?
4. Has the law firm developed a better understanding so that future transactions would be improved?

C. Service
1. Was the service provided skilful and professional?
2. Was the service provided reliable and responsive?
3. Were the documents accurate and of high quality?
4. Was supervision effective with clear points of contact?

D. Co-operation and trust
1. Did the law firm build a relationship of trust?
2. Could our personnel have been used more effectively?
3. How well did the law firm explain the steps to be taken?
4. How could communication have been improved?

E. Continuous improvement

1. What could the law firm have done better?
2. What could we have done better?
3. What should the law firm do differently next time?
4. What should we do differently next time?

Document 16 – drafting notes

1. Decide what questions are appropriate to your business or organisation for inclusion in this questionnaire.
2. Use your protocol or contract or letter of instruction and your key performance indicators as a basis.
3. Tell your law firms what criteria they will be judged on before, rather than after, the event. The aim is to help them improve, not to blame or catch them out.
4. Ensure that the questionnaire is widely distributed among those involved in the particular transaction.

Document 17
Breaking up is hard to do

Law Society rules and regulations

Sections 12.03 and 12.12 (Termination of the Retainer) state that 'a solicitor must not terminate his/her retainer with a client except for good reason and upon reasonable notice'. Good reason for not acting or continuing to act includes circumstances in which:

- a solicitor has insufficient time, experience or skill to deal with instructions
- a solicitor would be in breach of the rules or principles of conduct
- a solicitor is unable to obtain clear instructions from the client
- there is a serious breakdown in confidence between the lawyer and the client
- there is a failure to make a payment on account in certain circumstances
- there may be reason to believe the client may be involved in money laundering.

In reality, relationship and financial reasons play a vital part – see below.

Survey by Begbies Traynor extracted from *The European Lawyer Magazine*

A 2004 survey by Begbies Traynor reveals the following:

- 83 per cent of senior city lawyers say it's important to 'ditch' certain accounts 'to help their firms to grow.' Fifteen per cent had released three or more clients over the previous twelve months.
- Almost one-third of those surveyed (200) said that the main reason for letting clients go was conflict of interest while 17 per cent cited 'the risk of a client damaging my firm's reputation' or 'the client being difficult to deal with'. Twelve per cent said that they had had to let a client go because 'the size of the fee didn't justify the work'.

- The easiest way to lose clients is to raise fees. In looking at new clients the size of the fee is most important, while for current clients 'a pleasant working relationship' was equally important.
- When it came to 'giving a client the shove' – 53 per cent preferred one-to-one discussions and 54 per cent said that email was the 'least professional way of terminating the relationship'.
- For those in private practice who are reading this it might be interesting to note that 43 per cent said that, in hindsight, terminating a client relationship had been a poor business decision.

(The above article first appeared in the *European Lawyer* magazine, issue 45, February 2005 www.europeanlawyer.co.uk)

Generally

Firms are becoming more business orientated and are analysing whether clients are likely to pay decent rates and act properly during the relationship. Today, firms do conduct a periodical client cull and reality check as an accepted routine of clearing out the database.

If they have clients who give their young associates a hard time, question and whittle down every bill, or are late paying – then the relationship just isn't worth the pain it causes. In-house lawyers would not put up with this nor would their organisations – so why would law firms?

On the other hand, a review can also show those who have been taken off a client list due to inactivity. This gives the firm a chance to analyse whether it should be courting these clients or formally terminating the relationship to avoid future conflicts of interest.

Document 18
Exit plan

1. Introduction

   This exit plan is intended to deal with the situation where issues arise between the organisation and one of our external law firms. It is designed to escalate and resolve issues wherever possible, and to deal with termination and transfer of obligations with the minimum of inconvenience to all parties should this not be possible.

2. Dealing with conflict

   A solicitor is entitled to terminate a retainer in very limited circumstances. Where conflicts arise they should be capable of being dealt with by discussion and are likely to lead to termination only in the most difficult of situations. However, it is not in the interests of the organisation or the solicitor to continue in a relationship which is not mutually advantageous.

   We will aim to deal with any conflict in a businesslike and commercial manner.

3. Complaint resolution

   If complaints arise either about the conduct of a law firm, or about the conduct of any of the organisation's staff toward the firm, they should be referred to the contact partner and to the General Counsel for resolution.

   If the contact partner and General Counsel are not able to resolve the matter within 28 days, they may – if they consider it appropriate – refer the matter to the organisation's chief executive and the law firm's senior partner for further consideration.

   If it is still not possible to resolve the situation, the following paragraph applies.

4. Termination

If either the organisation or the law firm wishes to terminate the law firm's retainer, then the following provisions will apply:

- the law firm should be asked to prepare a list of all matters being undertaken
- it should also be asked to prepare a handover note for each matter setting out details of the matter, the present position, the agreed strategy and the next steps, together with any key dates
- a combined list of key dates should be prepared and held by the General Counsel
- the General Counsel will nominate an alternative firm or internal lawyer, and will arrange for the matters to be handed over
- there will be regular handover meetings between the General Counsel and the new law firm or internal lawyer.

5. Ownership of materials

The General Counsel will arrange that any necessary software licences are obtained to deal with continued use of materials in electronic format.

6. Personnel

It is not the policy of the organisation to agree to any limitations on the transfer of employees from external providers to the organisation, nor to agree to pay compensation in those circumstances.

7. Queries

Any queries should be addressed to the General Counsel.

[Date]

[Originator]

Further reading and resources

Networking groups

Association of Corporate Counsel (www.acca.com)
CLO (Chief Legal Officer Programme) (www.cloprogramme.com)
Commerce and Industry Group (www.cigroup.org.uk)
GC100 (for the FTSE 100)
General Counsel Roundtable (www.generalcounselroundtable.com)
Institute of Chartered Secretaries and Administrators (www.icsa.org)
Institute of Paralegals (www.InstituteofParalegals.org)

The Carillion Legal Network – member firms

Ashurst – www.ashurst.com
Clarkslegal LLP – www.clarkslegal.com
CMS Cameron McKenna – www.law-now.com
Dickinson Dees – www.dickinson-dees.com
DLA Piper Rudnick Gray Cary UK LLP – www.dlapiper.com
fbc – www.fbcsolicitors.com
Linklaters – www.linklaters.com
MacRoberts – www.macroberts.com
Pinsent Masons – www.pinsentmasons.com
Reynolds Porter Chamberlain – www.rpc.co.uk
Sacker and Partners – www.sackers.com
Slaughter and May – www.slaughterandmay.com
White and Case – www.whitecase.com

Further reading

Adams, Scott, *Dogbert's Top Secret Management Handbook*, Boxtree, 1997
Baggett, Byrd, *Dare to Lead*, Cumberland House Publishing, 2004
Fisher, Roger and Sharp, Alan, *Getting it Done*, HarperCollins, 1998

Forsyth, Patrick, *Business Planning*, Capstone, 2002

Gilbert, Paul, *Head2Head*, Author Publishing Limited, 2002

Heller, Robert, *Communicate Clearly (Essential Managers Series)*, Dorling Kindersley, 1999

Heller, Robert, *How to Delegate (Essential Managers Series)*, Dorling Kindersley, 1999

Honey, Peter, *101 Ways to Develop Your People Without Really Trying*, Peter Honey Publications, 1994

Honey, Peter, *Explore Your Values*, Peter Honey Publications, 2000

Jeffries, Susan, *Feel the Fear (and do it anyway)*, Arrow, 1991

McDermot, Ian and Jago, Wendy, *The NLP Coach*, Piatkus, 2001

Maister, David M. et al, *The Trusted Advisor*, Free Press, 2000

Maister, David M., *Practice What You Preach*, Free Press, 2001

Maister, David M., *True Professionalism*, Free Press, 1997

Maslow, A. H., *Motivation and Personality*, Harper, New York, 1954

Mayson, Stephen, *Making Sense of Law Firms*, Blackstone Press, 1997

Speechly, Chris and Wheatley, Ruth, *Developing a Culture for Diversity*, Institute of Management, Hodder and Stoughton, 2001

Templar, Richard, *The Rules of Management*, Pearson Prentice Hall Business, 2005

The Competitive Edge – The Growing Power of the DuPont Legal Model

Thomas, Neil and Adair, John Eric, *Teambuilding and Motivation*, Thorogood, 2004

Thomson, Larry A., *Shine*, McGraw Hill, 2005

Whitmore, Sir John, *Coaching for Performance*, Nicholas Brealey Publishing, 2003

Chambers Legal Directories: The UK Guide
                                The Global Guide
                                The USA Guide

Corporate Governance Committee, *Reconciling the Irreconcilable*, published by C & I Group Services, 2004

Corporate Governance Committee, *A Fine Line*, published by C & I Group Services, 2006

The Guide to the Professional Conduct of Solicitors, 8th edition, The Law Society

Resources

Beyond *the* Brief – www.beyondthebrief.com
  A professional development and training consultancy specialising in
  competency development for lawyers.
Chambers – publishers of the Chambers Legal Directory series
  www.chambersandpartners.com
First Law – a specialist consultancy dealing with law firm panel reviews –
  www.firstlaw.co.uk
International Law Office – www.internationallawoffice.com
Law Department Net – www.lawdepartment.net
Legal 500 – www.legal500.com
Legal Week – www.Legalweek.com
Martindale – www.martindale.com
The Lawyer – www.thelawyer.com

Index